PLANNING AND HMOs

Insights into Planning Rules and Planning Appeals for HMO Landlords

C. J. Haliburton

BA DMS Cert Ed and landlord with over 100 HMOs

www.hmodaddy.com

Copyright 2014 C. J. Haliburton

www.hmodaddy.com

The moral right of the author has been asserted.

All rights reserved. Apart from any fair dealing for the purposes of research or private study, or criticism or review, as permitted under the Copyright, Designs and Patents Act 1988, this publication may only be reproduced, stored or transmitted, in any form or by any means, with the prior permission in writing of the copyright owner, or in the case of the reprographic reproduction in accordance with the terms of licences issued by the Copyright Licensing Agency. Enquiries concerning reproduction outside those terms should be sent to the publisher.

HMO Daddy
14 Walsall Road
Wednesbury
West Midlands
WS10 9JL

Print Edition

ISBN: 978-1-326-12451-9

British Library Cataloguing in Publication Data.

A catalogue record for this book is available from the British Library.

Cover design, editing and formatting by Oxford Literary Consultancy.

Contents

Introduction 5
1: Outline 7
2: The Current Position 10
3: Actual Use 14
4: Sui Generis HMOs 16
5: Article 4 Direction 17
6: Parking 18
7: Planners 25
8: Getting Help 30
9: More Than Six Occupiers 32
10: Self-Contained Studios 34
11: Pre-2010 HMOs and Sui Generis HMOs 37
12: C4 HMOs and Permitted Development Rights ... 39
13: Established Use 42
14: Planning Contravention Notice (PNC) 43
15: Certificates of Lawfulness 45
16: Getting Planning Permission 47
17: Planning Committees 49
18: Licensing 50
19: Offices and Shops 52
20: Building Control 54

21: Council Tax 55

22: Planning Enforcement 61

23: Complaints to the Planning Department 65

24: Resolving Planning Problems 69

25: Why the Obscurity with Planning? 71

26: Should I Buy in an Article 4 Area? 75

Appendix i 81

Appendix ii 97

The Author 145

I Want to Hear from You 146

Introduction

The situation relating to HMOs is going to be one of the scandals of the late part of the last century and the early part of this century - not only with planning, but also in relation to the HMO property standards. So much is so wrong with the law and it is often vigorously enforced against landlords by those who know or should know better. HMO landlords are providing low-cost flexible housing so desperately needed by society often to vulnerable tenants, and HMO landlords deserve far better treatment, support and encouragement than they are currently given. I am not in any way condoning bad landlords, whatever that means. The balance is wrong and so little is said about the damage some tenants cause to the landlord's property, the problem over rent arrears and evicting bad tenants. Landlords are more the victims than the problem.

I have written this for the brave souls who dare to provide HMO housing and need a guide to the system. Do not expect much help or support from the authorities, even though you are on the side of the angels. I would urge HMO landlords to always fight if your council tries to stop you providing good quality HMO accommodation. If you stand up to the authorities you will be surprised how rarely the council will follow through and, if they do, how often they lose.

STAND UP TO THE PLANNERS!

1
Outline

The planning rules regarding Houses in Multiple Occupation (HMOs) are something that anyone who wishes to become an HMO landlord, or desires to increase their portfolio, should know and understand. In this business, it is of how rigorously the rules are enforced and interpreted. If you have a good grasp of the rules and are not easily intimidated by officials, you can do a lot more than you think or what the officials will admit you can do. Look at what travellers have done with the land they have purchased in the areas of the green belt to see how good planning enforcement is when people are determined to stand up to the planning system. I am not supporting such behaviour, but I can see little harm in providing low-cost flexible housing for working tenants. If you propose to house unemployed, (also known as DSS or LHA) tenants, then that is a different matter, as some of the unemployed can cause serious problems for neighbours.

Normally, if there are no complaints from 'concerned citizens', no one from the planning department will bother you. If this goes on for ten years, then you are probably in the clear. This is because ten years is the timeframe in which enforcement must take place for change of use, or four years if you have converted the property into separate dwellings, i.e. flats, small self-contained units or converted a building in the garden into a small house. You may need to prove it, keep date-stamped photographs, utility bills (if any) and tenancy agreements.

With most planning, it is not generally understood that it is not a criminal or a civil offence to do something without having planning permission. From the way some people react you would think it was a crime not to have planning permission. The council can only stop you if they can, in effect, prove that you would not have got planning permission in the first place. The paradox in planning is that if you would get planning permission, you don't need to apply for it. Breach of planning only becomes a criminal matter if the council takes enforcement action that you can appeal against. If you win you are in the clear, and if you lose you must stop using the property as you are. It is not a crime until an enforcement order is made and you break the order. You may wonder why anyone bothers to apply for planning permission for minor matters.

Since 2010, you do not need planning permission to change a house or flat into an HMO as the new Class C4 use allows up to six people to occupy a property providing they are sharing.* There could even be more than six people if the planners are unable to show that more than six would make a material difference. Also, if the house is large then it could be argued that it can be occupied by a large family of more than six people. The planning decision should be based on the size of the property and the impact of the occupation that more than six will have on the local amenities, e.g. schools, doctors, etc. The up-to-six-tenants rule is not as black and white as many see it. You can have more than six tenants without planning permission.

Planning officers normally take no action if the property has communal facilities, especially a kitchen, and has no more than six bedrooms, which they will 'assume' accommodate one person per room. En-suites do not, in my experience, cause concern to the planners so all the rooms can be en-suite.

Some planning officers like to see a communal lounge or at least a kitchen large enough to act as a breakfast kitchen.

Please appreciate that planning is totally separate from HMO Licensing (see Chapter 18), and has little connection with Building Control (see Chapter 20). You can license a property that should have but does not have planning permission. Some councils have a policy of not involving their planning departments in their decision to grant a license - and good for them! The result is that you could have the absurd situation of having a licensed HMO that the planners will not like, just hope they do not find out about it.

*Except where Article 4 Directions have been introduced (see Chapter 5.)

2
The Current Position

I am envious of the late comers, and by that I mean those who started HMOs after 2010. The government changed planning rules relating to HMO clarifying, or if you prefer allowing, the operation of an HMO without the prospect of having to have planning permission.

Before 2010, the planning situation was a grey area. With planning, nearly all property use is given a use class category. In the case of residential use, it is called C3, and prior to 2010 it was defined as:

Use as a dwelling (whether or not as a sole or main residence)

A. By a single person or by any number of persons living together as a family, or
B. By not more than six residents living together as a single household, including a household where care is provided for residents.

Normally, you need planning permission to change use categories, but not always. In 2010, a new use class was introduced, C4. This allowed HMOs with up to six people. The 'b' sub-section 'not more than six residents living as a single household' criteria was changed in the C3 use class and a new sub-section added to the C3 use. The new definition of C3 is given below:

C3 Dwelling Houses

I. A dwelling house, used by a single person or by people to be regarded as forming a single household.
II. Not more than six residents living together as a single household where care is provided for residents.
III. Not more than six residents living together as a single household where no care is provided to residents (other than a use within Class C4).

For most councils, if a house was let to six people in 2010, it became a C4 HMO and did not need consent. There is no need for planning permission to move between C3 and C4 use unless an Article 4 Direction applies to the area (see Chapter 5). Above six occupiers does not have a use category and is known as 'Sui Generis HMOs', but see Chapter 4. The definition of a Class C4 is given below:

C4 Houses in Multiple Occupation

Use of a dwelling house by not more than six residents as a 'house in multiple occupation'

If you, like me, wonder what the difference is between C3 (c) and C4, you are not alone. The ministerial guidance given states that the same definition of an HMO is to be used as within the Housing Act 2004 (see Appendix). The definition of an HMO within the Housing Act, if I may keep it simple, is that an HMO has to have more than two occupiers who are using the property as their main residence and are living separately i.e. not a couple or blood related. If there are lodgers, then occupied by three or more lodgers in addition to the resident landlord and his family. I will give a few examples to clarify:

Example 1

A couple of either sex, with or without children of the couple, plus a lodger – not an HMO, even though there are three or more persons occupying the house. The couple are in a relationship and you need more than two lodgers to make it licensable.

Example 2

Brothers/sisters/cousins, aunty, uncle living together – not an HMO even if more than two or six, as they are related by blood.

Example 3

A house adapted as an HMO but occupied by a family – not an HMO, even though the building looks like an HMO.

Note also that the same ministerial guidance, (see Appendix i), states that even though the word 'dwelling house' is used, the C4 definition also applies to flats (para 7). You, like me, may ask why did it not say so. Ministerial guidance is, by the way, not law. It is ultimately for the courts to decide. In this situation the HMO landlord just gets on with it. If you wait for clarification then you will not do anything. If you think planning law is bad try Housing Standards, another hurdle that the HMO landlord has to overcome. Housing standards can be made up, changed, ignored, applied and varied, and all in the same sentence.

3
Actual Use

You need to appreciate that it is not what the house or flat can accommodate, it is only its actual use that planners can action. Therefore, a ten-bedroom property that is only occupied by up to six persons not living as a family is definitely not a planning matter. Then again, even if more than six occupy it, it may not be a planning matter. (See Introduction above and Chapter 9 below.) It is not the intention that matters with planning, only actual use that can be enforced against.

Some HMO landlords have been known to start up an HMO and keep the numbers to six. Once the council's interest has passed, they increase the number of occupiers and who can blame them? It is not a crime unless the property is licensed, (see Chapter 18). The worst that can happen is that they can be made to return the property back to use by six occupiers. I should add that you have to be meticulous over all your dealings. Some councils, if they can't challenge you using planning law will try other ways, including housing standards, council tax, housing benefit, building control, waste collection (some councils are alleging that HMOs are not entitled to a waste collection even though they pay council tax), and report to your lender that you are using the property as an HMO. Not a problem if you are allowed to use the property as an HMO within your mortgage conditions. In short they can be evil. I would also not be surprised if they do not report you to the HMRC, but the HMRC do not tell you about reports while other departments often do.

4
Sui Generis HMOs

A Sui Generis HMO may need planning permission. A Sui Generis HMO is, since 2010, one that does not fit into the definition of class C4 use, i.e. it has more than six occupiers. (Please see Chapter 9.) Pre-2010 there was considerable variation by different councils as to how to distinguish between living as a household, i.e. C3, and not living as a household. The result was that planning could be used to prevent properties being rented out for shared occupation, as it was alleged the property use did not fit into the C3 use class. While planners have said they could not identify any logical or rational distinction between six living as a household and those not doing so, they declined to enforce, often also saying there was a need for such housing.

Beware that some, not many, councils have introduced an Article 4 Direction, (see Chapter 5) which effectively stops a property being let to more than two unrelated persons, but that would not stop me arguing C3 (c) use if I was in such a situation (see Chapter 2). In a storm take advantage of what you can.

5
Article 4 Direction

In October 2010, the government introduced a Permitted Development Right that allowed properties to move between C3 use class, i.e. living as a family, and C4 HMO, i.e. up to six persons sharing, without planning permission. However, councils could adopt, after following a lengthy procedure, an Article 4 Direction that removed this right, so all HMOs would need planning permission and/or to stop them moving between C3 and C4. Some councils have now adopted this restrictive policy across quite large areas, and not just a few streets, e.g. Oxford, Belfast, Newham and Leeds, to name just a few councils. Any property being used as a C4 HMO prior to an Article 4 area being adopted should be immune from enforcement action, but some authorities are not taking this view or are demanding proof of established use, (see Chapter 13).

All the HMO landlord can do with such an anti-HMO council is to stand their ground and see if the council takes enforcement action and appeal (see Chapter 21}. Like most bullies, if you stand up to them they will usually back off.

6
Parking

One of the favourite grounds for objecting to the grant of planning for HMOs is the lack of provision of parking, yet rarely is this successfully challenged. It takes balls to challenge this ground and success is assured. I do wonder how planners justify themselves using this objection when it rarely stands up on appeal. I have heard of planners stating that each room should have parking space for 1.5 cars. The same planners will then acknowledge that someone living in an HMO is very unlikely to own a car, never mind one-and-a-half cars each. My research shows it is about one in six tenants in an HMO that owns a car.

When challenged why they are demanding so much parking, planners will refer to guidance provided for flats. An HMO is not a flat.

The government in Planning Policy Guidance (PGG13) http://www.ice.org.uk/getattachment/42fd0f44-a93a-4cbc-bacb-d904727ece87/Planning-Policy-Guidance-13--Transportation-(PPG13.aspx at paragraph 8 states that in areas where there are good transport links, the rules on parking could be relaxed. It goes even further and says that it was for the developer to decide if they wished to provide parking or not.

I have attached a summary of the relevant part of PPG13 at the end. Like so much in PPGs, this is conveniently ignored by planners when it suits them. On the other hand, in some city centres planners have refused planning applications where developers have provided parking, saying they want to discourage car use in the city centre. In other words, the planners can make it up as they want.

I have had two planning appeals where the planning inspectors have dismissed the councils' demands for parking. On the third appeal they stated that, as they had had their demands for parking rejected twice, they did not want to insist on parking for a third time and lose on that ground.

One of those decisions was 41 Westbourne Road.

The 41 Westbourne Road decision can also be found at: http://www.pcs.planningportal.gov.uk/pcsportal/fscdav/READONLY?OBJ=COO.2036.300.12.765333&NAME=/Decision.pdf. The relevant paragraphs relating to parking are 30-32.

Other case studies from my files are:

1.   261 Walsall Road, Walsall:

http://www2.walsall.gov.uk/CMISWebPublic/Binary.ashx?Document=5768

The degree to which the occupiers of an HMO will generate parking has also been explored. In this case, the risk of parking from the client group is modest. The enforcement authority should be rescinded.

2.   33 Walsall St, Walsall:

http://www2.walsall.gov.uk/CMISWebPublic/Binary.ashx?Document=5768

There is no parking, however there is adequate amenity provision as there is a rear garden. It is considered that due to the size of this detached property that its conversion to flats may be acceptable even though there is no parking. It would be difficult to re-use this property for a suitable purpose which did not require parking

3.   12 Walsall Road, Darlaston:

I quote the inspector comment regarding parking:

Car parking provision:

16. No off-street parking is provided within the site. Policy T13 of the UDP requires 1.5 spaces per unit. The additional 4 units would therefore require 6 spaces to meet the relevant policy requirements. I was referred to the advice in the "Residential Car Parking Research-May 2007" (the Research) published by the Department for Communities and Local Government. This explains that dwelling size and type are major factors in determining car ownership levels. Tenure is another influence on household car ownership levels. The research indicates that the occupiers of the type of accommodation that is the subject of this appeal are unlikely to own a car. The appellant indicates that only one of the tenants currently occupying the development owns a car and that may not still be the case now. This reflects the findings of the research. Planning Policy Guidance Note 13 seeks to promote modes of transport other than the private car. I am mindful that the appeal site is within the District Centre location with a good range of services and facilities within walking distance and is well served by public transport. There is an unrestricted car park to the rear of the site.

17. To conclude on this issue, whilst I consider that the development does not comply with the car park standard set out in the UDP, I consider the development is unlikely to generate demand for 6 additional off-street parking spaces. Furthermore, I consider the development would not unduly prejudice highway safety as a result of lack of off-street parking within the site. For the reason set out I am satisfied parking is available.

PPGs

The PPG's can be found on the government website at:

http://www.ice.org.uk/getattachment/42fd0f44-a93a-4cbc-bacb-d904727ece87/Planning-Policy-Guidance-13--Transportation-(PPG13.aspx

A commentary on PPG13 has been produced by the Institute of Civil Engineers and the relevant parts are quoted below:

Car Parking

The availability of parking places may have a greater effect on choice of transport mode than the quality of public transport provided. Car parking policies should be laid down in the Regional Planning Guidance to avoid competition between adjacent authorities. Local plans should give minimum and maximum standards for parking provision across a broad range of types of development and locations.

Local planning authorities should:

- *adopt reduced requirements for parking at locations where access by other means of transport is good*
- *waive requirements for off-street residential parking where necessary to obtain high density developments in areas with good non-car access*
- *keep parking requirements to an operational minimum*
- *not disadvantage central areas by fulsome parking provision at peripheral office and retail developments*

On-street parking measures should be adopted which complement land-use policies and off-street parking policies.

Local Authorities can apply for Special Parking Areas.

Redevelopment of existing private parking should be encouraged to meet the revised standards. Planning permission for public and private car parks which do not meet the strategic aims of the plan should be refused.

Commuted payments for measures assisting public transport, walking and cycling, should be considered instead of payments for the supply of off-site parking.

Other useful links:

1) http://www2.walsall.gov.uk/CMISWebPublic/Binary.ashx?Document=4645

The need for the provision of parking for HMOs has also recently diminished due to the recently revised guidance in PPG13, whereby parking provision has been relaxed. This is particularly so in HMOs where car ownership might be low. It is possible that the success rate for the council would be low at appeal if lack of car parking spaces was the only reason for refusal. Where properties are located near to local transport links and are in town centres, this may be sufficient to overcome the parking objections. However, where on-road parking is already limited and the intensive use of housing in such areas would lead to exacerbation of the problems, then this could be a reason to refuse and enforce. This is particularly so as planning conditions cannot be used to restrict car ownership and therefore, in some cases, parking objections may be used as valid reasons for taking enforcement action.

2) Caerphilly, South Wales guidance.

http://www.caerphilly.gov.uk/pdf/Environment_Planning/Supplementary-planning-guidance/LDP5-car-parking-standards.pdf

(c) Conversion of a large 3-storey 5-bedroomed Victorian house to three one-bedroomed flats (in Zone 3)

The parking requirement for the original house is three parking spaces, but given the age of the property, these may not actually be present.

The parking requirement for the flats is one space per bedroom. Three parking spaces are therefore required in theory. These should, if possible, be provided at the rear of the premises. If the site has no existing parking, the conversion will not require any, although it would be desirable to gain these parking spaces. If the site is too small to accommodate three cars and the house fronts a local road that is not a bus route, and kerbside parking pressure is not evident, then an allowance of on-street parking immediately outside may be possible. Local circumstances should always dictate the approach to be taken.

7
Planners

Prior to April 2010, up to six unrelated occupiers 'living as a household' was considered to still be a dwelling (C3), and did not need planning permission providing they lived as a household. The meaning of household was subject to much argument. Houses or rooms let to people living independently of each other (i.e. they were not considered a household) did not fall within a use class. These were called Sui Generis HMOs, as there was no use category for a property being used residentially outside class C3 use. I suspect this was because the legislators probably thought C3 covered all residential use and did not appreciate that houses and flats could be used differently. If they had, I believe they would have included it in the C3 use. The legislators have effectively done this now to a limited degree by introducing the new class C3 (c) definition and the C4 classification. From a planning point of view, a property can be switched between family and HMO use and vice-versa without restriction or any formality or notice except in an Article 4 area, (see Chapter 5).

When the Housing Act 2004 was introduced, the Government talked about a light touch approach, saying that one day a property could be used by a family and the next as an HMO with very little needing to be done. In many areas, this has not proved to be the case. Many thousands of pounds need to be spent, mainly on fire precautions to the property, to make it suitable for HMO use. If the works are not done the landlord could be served with improvements notices and be liable to prosecution for having an unsafe HMO.

The C4 classification in the ministerial guidance states 'between 3 to 6 unrelated individuals who share basic amenities'. So far, to my knowledge, no council has picked up on the meaning of 'share'. Does this mean sharing the same house, or must there be an element of communal sharing such as a kitchen or bathroom?

The definition of an HMO is now the same as for the Housing Act 2004, which talks about occupation. So why add the word 'share'?

In law, every word must be given a meaning and yet it appears that 'share' does not add anything to the definition of C4. Does it only mean occupying. This confusion may cause problems with the studio-style HMOs, where the tenant has their own en-suite and kitchenette, the style provided in, usually, the more upmarket HMOs (see Chapter 10).

Planners, I find, are strange people and some, but by no means all, see themselves as upholders of the law with total disregard for the consequences of what they do, or are just power-hungry and want to split hairs to exert their authority. A few believe that a complaint about your property means you are doing something wrong, and assume the complainer is right and you must stop using your property as an HMO and let it to a family or, preferably, it should not be let but owner-occupied.

I have great sympathy with many neighbours and believe we, as landlords, have a duty to take care in selecting and positioning HMOs and appropriate tenants, i.e. not to let an HMO to the unemployed (also known as DSS or LHA tenants), next to owner-occupied family properties. The same goes for single-let properties. I have seen too many blocks of flats wrecked by one bad family, with out-of-control children and animals. The existing law is a very blunt instrument in trying to control such behaviour, and with single-lets there is absolutely no control over who a landlord may let to. With HMOs the only control now, unless it is an Article 4 area, is the number of tenants.

No one in our politically correct world talks about tenant types, i.e. professional, working, and DSS/LHA tenants. HMO lets to professionals, or working tenants, rarely cause any problems. It is the DSS/LHA end of the market that can cause so many problems for neighbours. Society has not addressed what we do with the dysfunctional sector. Councils, such as Newham, have just shipped them out to other areas to no doubt reek mayhem there. I would urge all prospective HMO landlords to site their HMOs carefully if they are planning to let to the unemployed.

I have little sympathy for those who want to do something about students. The boat has sailed on this one. The student areas already exist and little can be done or, I believe, should be done about changing it.

It is not widely appreciated that the reason why planning legislation was introduced by the Labour government after the Second World War was to stop landowners profiting from the use of their land. The government almost destroyed the private rented sector with their anti-landlord legislation, and a side effect was to create and sustain a bureaucracy or industry of local authority planners and consultants. Neither of these two groups are going to argue they are of little use or a problem for society. You only have to read a few Planning Policy Guidelines (PPGs), available free by download on the website, www.planningpolicyguidelines.co.uk, to realise that the government is continually being frustrated by overzealous local authority planners. PPG's are guidance that government gives to planners as to how they should be interpreting the planning rules.

Therefore, do not expect some planners to show any concern for the wider issues (such as the need for low-cost, affordable, flexible housing that HMOs provide or even the need for housing), as they are just obsessed with the rules. Even though planners have considerable latitude in the interpretation and application of the rules, they have often been known to go much further and distort and misrepresent their authority and the law and totally ignore PPGs. I have even been told by a local authority planner many years ago that certain PPGs do not apply as they are being rewritten. They still have not been rewritten.

As an HMO landlord, you need to know the planning rules and be prepared to defend yourself against those planners who exceed their authority. If a landlord was to so misrepresent themselves in the same way, they would leave themselves open to a criminal action for fraud and be severely fined and maybe imprisoned. It is a strange society we live in.

While I am at it, you may reflect that most of the examples of wonderful architecture were created pre-planning legislation and most of the awful examples are post-planning, i.e. since 1948. I question whether planners serve any useful purpose in our society.

8
Getting Help

It is one of many perversities of this business that we, as HMO landlords, are constantly told by bodies who profess to support us to engage with the regulators when we are not sure what to do. Yet the regulators can be our worst enemies. I engage with the regulators if I have to, initially in a general manner, and if the advice resonates with what I want I will make it specific and name the property I have concerns about. Would you ask the devil for advice about how not to sin? Unfortunately there are very few angels out there to ask and get impartial advice from.

I spent thousands of pounds getting advice on planning, and then realised I could have done as well, if not better, myself. Even with the best advice, whatever that is, you need to make your own decision to fight or give in. Consultants are mainly concerned with fees and their liability – your best interest is a low priority. With planners I would consider it is always worth fighting, even with what planning consultants consider are hopeless cases. But don't be disappointed if with good cases you lose – planning is like that. The inexperienced believe that there are laws that experts only understand, when the reality is that planning is largely a game of hide and seek. If you are caught, then it becomes a game of bluff, patience, gamesmanship and nerve. There is little justice and you need a lot of luck. HMO landlords exist at the whim or inertia of your council. If your council is prepared to distort the truth, deceive and throw enormous resources into stopping you, they are more likely to succeed. But there is no guarantee they will succeed, as I have shown.

It is a shame but perfectly understandable if most landlords just give up, considering it is not worth the fight – it is the stress and uncertainly of it all that I find most landlords cannot cope with. It is like living with an unexploded time bomb in your back garden. You learn to live with it just as those who live in earthquake or tsunami regions live with the fear of earthquakes or tsunamis.

9
More Than Six Occupiers

The difference between C4, which does not need planning permission, and a Sui Generis HMO, which needs planning permission, is not as clear cut as first appears. Class C4 use on the face of it suggests that this relates to a property with three to six unrelated occupiers and that seven or more is a Sui Generis HMO. This is not strictly true as planning legislation only requires planning approval if there is 'a material difference'. Adding a seventh or eighth person to your HMO will not necessarily make the use so different that it is no longer a C4 HMO. If you read the circular 08/2010 published by the Department of Communities and Local Government in November 2010 at Schedule A, para 17, it clearly states this (see Appendix i). Some planning officers only believe the rules apply to you and not to them and para 17 does not apply, so be prepared to have to stand your ground when they try to bully you into reducing the number of occupants in your HMO or having to apply for planning permission if you have more than six occupiers.

Beware that if you do apply for planning permission for a Sui Generis HMO you will need planning permission to return it back to a C3 residence. This may not be forthcoming. In London, for example, the local authorities say they are against the loss of HMO accommodation and refuse permission, so possibly depriving the owner of a substantial increase in the value the property would command as a single residence in London. However, in other parts of the country the need for HMO accommodation is ignored, and landlords were, pre-2010, forced to turn their HMOs back into single residences and to reduce occupation. Would I be cynical if I suggest that this was more to do with the fact that landlords were profiting from the HMO use rather than concerns over the need for low-cost flexible housing?

10
Self-Contained Studios

The definition of a C4 HMO is stated to be the same as the definition of an HMO in the 2004 Housing Act. An HMO can include the traditional shared accommodation, or rooms, with either or both en-suite and kitchen facilities, with or without shared lounges and/or shared kitchens and/or bathrooms. Some councils seek planning applications for the change of use of each self-contained room to a C3 dwelling. Whether this is a correct interpretation of the legislation is in dispute. I would supply a shared kitchen and restrict any separate cooking facilities in the rooms to tea making for planning purposes to avoid possible problems. Supplying en-suites rarely causes a problem from the planning point of view, it is only when you try and add cooking facilities, especially if there is no shared kitchen. However, solving one problem may create another in that if the property is three storeys or more, this may make it licensable if there are five or more occupiers (see Chapter 17).

Planning permission is only required for the building as a single HMO if it is for more than six occupiers, or possibly seven or eight occupiers, (see above).

More than six occupiers, or in an area with an Article 4 Direction, it is a debatable point if permission is required for conversion of a dwelling for up to six, or possibly more, self-contained studios, especially if there is a shared kitchen. In other words, when does it stop being an HMO and become a flat? I strongly suspect a property can be an HMO and, if sufficiently self-contained, become a separate dwelling from a planning perspective and so require planning permission.

From the Housing Act 2004 perspective, a flat is not an HMO if it is self-contained and complies with the Building Regulations 1991. Obviously, if Building Regulations had been applied for and obtained, this is then clear-cut. The reality is that in the messy world of HMOs, most HMO conversions were done without Building Regulations approval. There is a presumption that if the 1991 Building Regulations had not been obtained, then it is an HMO. It would be for the landlord to prove that the 1991 Building Regulations were complied with by getting a certificate from a suitably qualified professional.

In planning terms, whether a property is self-contained or not is a matter of fact, not building control approval, and after four years established use will apply (see Chapter 12). Smart operators are seeking out old HMOs that have become, over the years, self-contained, and turning them into flats. In such circumstances there is no need for planning and building control approval. Where the market for flats has allowed it, selling the flats off at substantial profit is all perfectly legal.

If you ask your planning department whether you need planning permission for something, or even your consultant, they will say it will not hurt to get planning permission and to not do so may incur you substantial costs. Local authority planning departments are desperate to increase their fee income as they are measured on income. The planning fee is usually the tip of the iceberg. Once you have added the cost of drawing-up plans and your consultant fees, you are looking at many thousands of pounds, never mind your time. Life was so much simpler when planning applications were free – planners did not want to hear from HMO landlords unless they had complaints about the HMO. Unfortunately, as with so much in this business, you have to make your own decisions if you are going to have any hope of making a viable business or a profit.

11
Pre-2010 HMOs and Sui Generis HMOs

What is now a Sui Generis HMO will need planning permission to return to a C3 residence, especially if planning permission as a Sui Generis HMO has been obtained or a certificate of lawfulness obtained. However, if planning permission has not been obtained, it has obtained this status by established use, (see Chapter 13). In practice, unless you flag it up I doubt anyone will realise that you need planning permission to turn back to a C3 residence. What the position is of properties that were occupied by six or less before 2010 is not clear, as pre-2010 it could be argued (very unlikely) they were Sui Generis HMOs and so would need planning permission to return to a C3 residence, even though post-2010 they could change back and forth between C3 and C4 as development permitted. The legislation, as with so much in the area of landlord law, is rarely thought through and, worse, the legislators have no awareness of the unintended consequences of what they are doing.

This area of planning is uncharted territory and very few planning enforcement officers or consultants have a clue about HMOs, never mind enforcement, and get it very wrong. The planning rules allow you to do far more than most people can imagine, if applied correctly. All this nonsense about beds in sheds – it could and probably is permitted development providing the persons in the sheds are part of the main household. There is nothing in planning that stops you having a child or your partner sleeping at the bottom of your garden providing they also inhabit the house. I hope I am not giving some of my readers ideas.

You are, within limits, allowed to build structures in your garden and use them as you wish, so long as the use is connected with the main residence. For example, office, garage, workshop, billiard room, Jacuzzi or playroom. The upset over sheds has a disturbing racist undertone. Would they be upset if they were occupied by children, pigeons or flowers instead of immigrants?

The fear is, without any research to verify it, that outbuildings are being used to house illegal immigrants and this has started what can only be described as a witch hunt and, unfortunately, HMO landlords are being entangled in it. Do we target motorists because bank robbers and drug dealers use cars? If you are in any doubt, I suggest you read *Dealing with Rogue Landlords* published by the DCLG (see Appendix ii). It is, on so many grounds, wrong and is probably one of the most bigoted publications I have ever read from a government department.

12
C4 HMOs and Permitted Development Rights

Permitted Development Rights (PDRs) are the ability to develop residential houses without planning permission. Within limits a house can be extended, a porch built, and outhouses can be built in the back garden, etc.

Unless the council has withdrawn Permitted Development Rights, the same rights that apply to houses also apply to C4 HMOs, though some councils dispute this. See the guidance the Planning Inspectorate have given to their planning appeal inspectors (attached at the end of this chapter), which clearly states that the HMO should benefit from Permitted Development Rights. However, when a council implement an Article 4 Direction any property classified as C4 will not have Permitted Development Rights.

Watch out for planning conditions when considering the conversion of garages to a room if the house is relatively new. The original planning permission for the property could contain restrictions that prevent garages being used for residential use. However, if you do make the change and no action is taken within ten years, you benefit from established use, (see Chapter 13).

With older properties, for example a pub where I used the flat above as an HMO, I had a planning enforcement officer say that the flat had restricted planning use so could only be occupied by those working in the pub and so I must make a planning application for the change of use. The pub had closed and had been empty for about ten years. I am not talking about ground floor use, what was the pub area, but the residential flat above. The planning enforcement officer was unable to produce any proof of this restriction, and neither could she, as the pub was built around 1900, forty years before any planning legislation was introduced and so no restriction could exist unless a planning application had been made after 1944 (when planning was introduced), which changed the pub or the flat's use. This is only a taste of what you have to put up with when you get embroiled with planners.

Once you go along the planning application route, the planners have enormous discretion as to what conditions they can impose. This is because opinions are subjective as to their idea of what is called 'amenity' or 'harm to the amenity'. This includes parking, bin and bicycle storage, garden space, noise, outlook, size of rooms or communal areas. The list is only limited by a planner's imagination.

The Planning Inspectorate

Advice produced by the Planning Inspectorate for use by its Inspectors – 15 January 2014

Houses in Multiple Occupation (HMOs) and Permitted Development Rights

1. The Town and Country Planning (General Permitted Development) Order 1995 (as amended) (GDPO) Schedule 2 Part 1 Class A grants certain permitted development rights to dwellinghouses.

2. Houses in Multiple Occupation, including those which fall within Class C4 can benefit from the permitted development rights granted to dwellinghouses by the GDPO. Class C4 use is defined as use of a dwellinghouse by not more than six residents as a "house in multiple occupation".[1]

3. The test for whether a property is eligible to use the permitted development right is whether it can be considered a "dwellinghouse" within the context of the GDPO. This will depend on the facts of the case.

4. Case law[2] has established that the distinctive characteristic of a "dwelling house" is its ability to afford to those who use it the facilities required for day-to-day private domestic existence. Whether a building is or is not a dwelling-house is a question of fact.

5. For the purposes of the GDPO a "dwellinghouse" does not include a building containing one or more flats, or a flat contained within such a building.

---

[1] Town and Country Planning (Use Classes) Order 1987 (as amended)
[2] *Gravesham Borough Council v The Secretary of State for the Environment and Michael W O'Brien* (1982) 47 P&CR 142 [1983] JPL 307

13
Established Use

If you have an HMO in an area covered by an Article 4 Direction with three tenants or more, or a Sui Generis HMO, you are immune from enforcement action after ten years' continuous use. The planning department cannot require an application or take enforcement action against HMOs after ten years continuous use, or maybe only four years if self-contained studios. This is known as established use.

Many flats, and to a lesser extent houses, vertically split as opposed to a horizontally split for flats, have been created by this means with no reference to planners. If they were done some time ago, they do not even need Building Control approval (see Chapter 20).

14
Planning Contravention Notice (PNC)

This is usually the second round of attack the planners use, if you do not roll over and do as they say. They can be quite intimidating and some appear to allege that you are doing something wrong and are subject to penalties, fines, etc. This, I believe, is wrong. Their function should be to identify ownership and use. I feel instinctively that there is something in terms of legal principles wrong with them as you have to incriminate yourself. This is against one of the fundamental principles of English Law, the right to silence, but planning contravention is not a crime until enforcement is taken.

It is, however, a crime not to complete and return the PCN, or to give incorrect information. I fill them in, date them on the penultimate day they give you to comply, hand deliver it to the planning department and get a receipt or email and send by post, i.e. always get proof of sending/delivery. In the early days when I was not used to the system I ignored the PNCs and all that happened was the planners wrote to me again. Do not assume your council will do the same.

If the information the PNC requires is to your advantage, i.e. you have operated the property as self-contained units for over four years, say so as it may help to prove established use, (see Chapter 13). The council will certainly use the PNC against you if you don't.

Most of the time I hear no more from the planners once I have completed and returned the PNC. In this situation, no news is good news. I have a dilemma when completing the PNC as to whether to address the planners' concerns and explain, if I can, why the use does not breach planning rules.

I have so far refrained from providing free education to the planners, but I am not sure this is the best approach. Then again by showing your defence at an early stage may strengthen the planners' position.

In conclusion, the PNC means nothing more than you have to fill it in, return it and wait, hopefully forever, for the next round.

15
Certificates of Lawfulness

If you are in an area with an Article 4 Direction in place and your house or flat was used by six persons before the adoption of the Article 4 Direction in the area, you should have a defence if the planners try to enforce. Many planners will tell you differently. The argument is whether an Article 4 Direction is retrospective and the presumption in law is that legislation is not retrospective.

If you wish to prove established use, you can apply for a certificate of lawfulness from the council's planning department. You will usually need to provide evidence of tenants being in occupation for ten years, or four years if self-contained, and maybe even continuously for that period.

Planning authorities vary considerably in their approach to providing certificates of lawfulness. The tip is to give as much information as possible, look at it from the planners' point of view. If they are given a 2-inch-thick file of documents to prove established use, they would have covered themselves if anyone checked, as opposed to a few sheets of paper. Some planning authorities are very pedantic, wanting documentary proof such as tenancy agreements, rent schedules, utility bills paid by tenants, statutory declarations and for you to prove continuous use for the whole period. Other planning authorities are very easily satisfied and probably grateful of the fee you are required to pay for the certificate of lawfulness, so they will grant them quite easily. A certificate of lawfulness is sometimes required by lenders and may be asked for by the purchaser if you sell your HMO.

16
Getting Planning Permission

If you apply for planning permission, the council will seek the views of local residents and most enforcement action is due to neighbour complaints. It is important that your tenants do not annoy their neighbours. Effectively monitor bin management, upkeep of gardens, noise, possible disturbance, parking use and all other issues.

If an application is required for an HMO, the council sometimes requires additional car parking, noise insulation, amenity space, contributions to space and trees, etc. Many of the councils have decided that only up to X% of HMOs will be allowed in an area, but no HMOs in terraced properties or next to each other, etc. If purchasing a property to be used as an HMO, check if or when Article 4 was introduced and the council's policies regarding HMOs.

Do not underestimate the challenge of getting consent for an HMO and consider purchasing a property that already has an established use, as the planning process has little rationality to it. Do not expect the planning inspectors (those who hear appeals against the refusal of planning permission) to be any more than rubber-stampers of your local planning committee. In this insane system there exists a breed of very expensive consultants who seem to be more successful than others that you may wish to use if you want to succeed in getting planning permission.

Appreciate that many of the demands or conditions planners impose are not valid and if challenged will disappear. I question the morality of such a profession, i.e. a council planner can raise objections which, if they are even only partially competent, they must know are irrelevant. I have had planning objections based on nothing more than they did not like me, as I did not apply for planning permission when it was questionable whether planning permission was required; that I house people from outside the area (foreigners); and I was in competition with the council housing department and operating for a profit. Luckily, the council did not succeed, but it cost me thousands of pounds to defend the case and took up a lot of my time.

So far there appears to be little evidence of much enforcement against Sui Generis HMOs, even in areas where Article 4 Directions have been introduced, so you would expect greater enforcement. Maybe the use of Article 4 coincided with the cutbacks in public spending and council planning departments do not have the staff to enforce. As the whole business of law enforcement seems to be without consistency or rationality, who knows? Anyone who is prosecuted could always argue (unsuccessfully) they have been victimised as over 99% of those who are also doing the same are not. Try driving at 70 miles per hour on the motorway and count how many drivers overtake you. Speeding drivers are said to kill (though the evidence is questionable) – HMOs do not.

17
Planning Committees

When making a planning application, should there be any dispute - for example a neighbour objects to you being allowed planning permission - then the matter has to, in most councils, be referred to the planning committee, which consists of locally elected councilors, i.e. amateur, unpaid elected officials. I suggest you attend a planning committee meeting at your local council to fully appreciate the kangaroo court style and braying donkey antics that go on in such committees. Many of the committee members have little grasp of planning law, do not read the applications, and start going on about social welfare or building control. A good chair can manipulate the committee to pass or refuse an application.

The current government has introduced the idea of localism and, even though you can appeal to the planning inspectorate, I am told the planning inspectors are now very reluctant to overrule planning committees. My view on planning inspectors has already been expressed, (see Chapter16). So even though things are far better than when I started, with the introduction of Class C4 use, in some respects it is worse as planning inspectors are even more inclined to rubber-stamp the council's decision than before.

18
Licensing

Licensing is the most misunderstood aspect of HMOs, including by many of those who are paid to apply licensing. Appreciate that planning control and HMO licensing are totally different. There is no connection between the two, you may need both, either or neither depending on your particular circumstances and council. Simply put, a license is required for HMOs if there are five or more unrelated occupiers over three storeys where there is any sharing of kitchens, toilets and/or bathrooms. Problems arise with this definition when you try to define storeys, sharing and occupiers, and apply the law to flats.

Planning used to be used as the authority's main weapon to stop landlords using a property as an HMO. Increasingly, it is now housing standards departments applying over-the-top amenity criteria, such as requiring individual bathrooms for each resident and excessive space standards. However, planning is still used as a weapon and many councils insist that you need planning permission before they will grant a license for an HMO in an Article 4 area or a Sui Generis HMO. This is incorrect and there are residential property decisions now called the First Tier Appeal Tribunals that support this, that licensing of an HMO is not connected in any way with planning. Yet planners and housing standard officers will allege differently and they say they are on the side of right and HMO landlords are the wrongdoers. In other words, they have to license you whether or not you have planning permission, though many council housing standard department will report you to the planning department or take as long as they want over granting a license. I have not had a license granted in anything less than twelve months. I don't mind how long they take as the length of the license, usually five years, runs from the month it is granted.

If your local authority is anti-HMO and knows about your HMO, it may be a good strategy to apply for a license by bringing the property into licensing if it has three or more storeys, for example counting the basement or loft, or letting to five or more tenants, if there is any doubt as to the planning position of your HMO as this makes it more difficult for the planners to take enforcement action. Council departments are supposed to work together yet the law often does not allow them to do so, and so the result is they can look stupid when they enforce against a licensed HMO, i.e. one department is giving what appears is permission while the other is trying to stop its use and, as I said above, they have to license you whether or not you have planning permission. I have never heard of a planning enforcement action against a licensed HMO, although it is not guaranteed that there will never be such action.

The same goes for grants, which you are unlikely to get in this financial climate, for taking tenants the council refers to you (best avoid as they are very difficult to manage) or using council bond schemes, etc. The more you can show you are operating in the open and engaging with your council the better, but it is in no way conclusive.

19
Offices and Shops

The current government has given a fantastic opportunity to investors if you understand that since 2013 an office can be converted into a C3 residence without planning permission, subject to prior approval covering flooding, highways and transport issues and contamination. Most local authorities have not set up any systems to deal with notification, so I presume you just drop them a line and get on with it.

As a C3 residence it appears that there is nothing to stop it being used as a C4 HMO. The ability to do this is time-limited, so take advantage while you can. Offices can often be bought at a fraction of the cost of the same residential space, another great opportunity for landlords, especially HMO landlords. My experience is that HMO tenants take little notice of the exterior of the property, it is the locality of the HMO and the facilities that attract. Offices that would not be suitable as flats or houses for family occupation will often be acceptable to HMO residents.

Since April 2014, the government has allowed small retail shops (up to 150 square metres) to be changed to residential use. Again, prior approval must be sought for which there is a fee of £80 to pay.

For further information see the government website:

SI2014No.564 (htt://www.legislation.gov.uk/uksi/2014/564/made), associated SI2014No.565 (http://www.

legislation.gov.uk/uksi/2014/565/contents/made) and related explanatory memorandum (http://legisation.gov.uk/uksi/2014/564/pdfs/uksiem 20140564 en.pdf).

20
Building Control

Building control operate separately and often independently of other council departments, including planning. Building control, like planners, are seeking to increase their income by insisting on building control applications. Not applying for building control approval when you should is a criminal offence, but they only have six months to prosecute. What would be considered as minor building works just a few years ago, and overlooked for building control purposes, may now result in prosecution if you do not apply for building control approval.

If you have done recent building works, i.e. within the last six months, which you are told by building control should have building control approval, apologise and say you did not realise, ask them what they would like you to do. Usually it is to apply for retrospective approval. I suggest you would be wise to comply as it may be cheaper in the long run than being prosecuted. I very much doubt that building control would show any interest in HMOs if fees were not involved, or in your HMO once you have paid the fee.

Building control has been partly privatised and you can appoint your own. You do not need to use the council's building control officers. Unlike planners, I have always found council building control officers very helpful, so it is a shame it was not the planners who were privatised.

21
Council Tax

The standards position with council tax is that the landlord is responsible for paying the council tax on an HMO. This is the law. However, there is nothing to stop the landlord passing this liability on to the tenant(s) within the tenancy agreement. Many HMO landlords do this and I suspect the council do not know the property is an HMO and think they are billing the tenant for the whole house or flat. Often the same is done with the utilities: the bills are put in the name of one lead tenant or a number of tenants, and the landlord leaves it to them to sort it out.

The reality is that as long as the bills are paid, no one usually cares. If the utilities are not paid, as long as a new liability is created (i.e. a new name is put as the current occupier), the gas and electric companies will bill the new name. If the bill remains unpaid, then the utility companies will fit prepay meters. Utility companies are not allowed to disconnect utilities from residential properties. The outstanding bill will be added to the prepay meter and, if there are new tenants, they will be charged for the old tenant's bill. When this happens, you will usually find it very hard to get the utility company to accept the new tenant is not liable. Though, strictly speaking, the supply of utilities with single-lets is down to the tenant, the tenant will complain to you and I have had tenants leave because the utility companies have charged for the outgoing tenant unpaid bill via the prepay meter and failed to remove the charge.

There is a different definition of an HMO for council tax purposes. An HMO for council tax purposes needs only to have two tenants, while for planning and Housing Act purposes it is three or more unrelated tenants occupying. However, I get the impression that council tax departments make it up as they go and, as long as they are paid, don't really care who is liable. There is an exception to this with joint tenancies. If the tenants are on one tenancy, they are liable for the council tax. If you have a problem getting this accepted, refer your council to the Shelter Guide – Guide to Housing Benefit and Council Tax Benefit – ISBN 19050181699781905018161 – Chapter 9.9 – 9.26, see extract at the end of the chapter.

Some enterprising landlords have managed to get the tenants responsible for council tax by using joint tenancies and still obtain the one room rate (or even the one bed rate if the room is sufficiently self-contained or they have exclusive use of two rooms) from housing benefit, where the tenants are claiming housing benefit. It seems that councils vary in their approach or even between landlords. Some housing benefit departments are under the erroneous view that the one bed rate for HB (often called the one bed flat rate) can only be paid if the tenant is liable for the council tax. This is incorrect, the one bed rate is paid for:

1. A flat
2. Exclusive use of room, bathroom and kitchen
3. Exclusive use of room, bathroom and have own cooking facilities
4. Exclusive use of two rooms, even though there is sharing

of kitchen or bathroom
5. Care leavers up to the age of 22, even if they live in a room in a shared house

Students are a special case in that if they are on a full-time course and the college issues a council tax exemption certificate, then the student is exempt from council tax. Where there is a shared house, i.e. an HMO, then ALL the occupiers must be students and have exemption certificates. In this case the landlord, who is usually responsible for paying the council tax, can be exempt from paying. However, if one of the students leaves the course and stays in occupation, the landlord will become liable for the council tax. If it is only one person in the house of otherwise exempt students, then the landlord can claim the one person reduction, i.e. 25%, in council tax, even though there are other students in the house.

Some council tax departments are now treating each room in an HMO as a separate dwelling for council tax purposes and charging each occupant council tax. The law is that the landlord of an HMO is usually the one liable for the council tax unless every room in the property is classified as a separate dwelling. The more self-contained the room is, i.e. has its own en-suite and/or kitchen, the greater the danger of the room being classified as a dwelling. The other term used is a 'heriditiment'. You can have a property where, say, two of the rooms are self-contained and the tenants have to pay their own council tax and you, as the landlord, are required to pay the council tax on the rest of the property. In effect the council is getting three times the council tax from a property for which they used to only get one council tax.

With most HMOs the property comprises of or a mixture of:

1. Rooms with shared kitchen and bathroom, no en-suite or cooking facilities in the rooms
2. Room or rooms with own en-suite and shared kitchen or kitchens for the whole house
3. Rooms with their own kitchens and shared bathroom or bathrooms for the whole house
4. All rooms with their own kitchen and en-suite, i.e. each room is self-contained but with a communal kitchen, bathroom or laundry room
5. All rooms with their own kitchen and en-suites, i.e. each room is self-contained

The further you move from (1) above, the more likely it is the council will separately band each room, i.e. decide it is a dwelling, but even in (5) above it is not always the case that each room will be classified as a separate dwelling. Some councils will want to see a property with a bathroom, more than one room and a separate kitchen before they will classify it as a dwelling, but again it is all down to the individual council.

As the law in this area is so vague and wide there is little you can do. Should a council decide that each room is a dwelling for council tax purposes, it removes from the landlord the obligation to pay the council tax on the property and places it on the tenant. The sweetness of the saving on council tax for the owner is tempered by the increased administration such a decision causes, due to having to notify the council every time a tenant leaves and a new tenant moves in, the charge to the owner during void periods, and increased cost and dissatisfaction caused to tenants.

In the few cases where the council tax department has separately banded each room in my properties, it has not made any difference to my tenants, possibly because many were LHA so had it paid for them. Working tenants appeared to ignore it and unfortunately just move when the council puts pressure on them to pay. I can foresee the prisons being filled in a few years by HMO tenants who had not paid their council tax, just as we had with poll tax dodgers. Why does the government never learn? I still charge the same rent as I did when I paid the council tax and to my endless amazement tenants do not seem to appreciate the difference. I have the same issue with utilities: tenants rarely appreciate me paying them.

There seems little rationality as to when the council apply a council tax charge to each room as opposed to the whole or part of the house. I suspect charging by the room happened in my properties when a tenant applied to pay council tax and the council just accepted their application. Usually, when I find out and ask for the council tax to be paid by me on the whole building as an HMO, the council change it back and I pay one council tax for the whole building. In other words, some councils leave it to the tenants and the owner to decide the position. If this is the case, it would be sensible to choose what liability suits you.

With regards to cost, unless the council tax charge for different bands varies enormously in your area, it will always cost in total far more to have each unit separately banded, even though most tenants will be able to claim the 25% single person discount as they live alone. Appreciate that the lowest council charge is Band A and this will be charged for a whole house and for a room in an HMO if the room is separately banded.

Example

Property with six rooms in my area: I pay about £1K in council tax for the whole house. If each room is separately banded for council tax, it will be 6 x £1K x 75%, i.e. 4.5 times the cost of the house.

To sum up, usually the landlords pay council tax or are legally responsible for the council tax. The tenant pays and is legally responsible for the council tax if the room(s) is/are separately banded. The council decides almost at their sole discretion whether the house is an HMO or the rooms are separate dwellings and so the tenant pays the council tax and a bill is issued for each room, usually band A, though occupiers of the room, if living alone, can claim 25% single person occupation discount. Councils will usually go along with what you want and treat a house as an HMO. If this is what you want or if the units are self-contained you can ask them to separately band them.

22
Planning Enforcement

The problem the planning enforcement officer (PEO) has is that if they believe a breach of planning law is taking place they should decide whether it is appropriate to take enforcement action. The criteria applied are down to each council. Most PEOs have an enormous amount of discretion or if they do not see things my way I would consider them to be totally out of control. In other words, when does unlimited discretion become total unreasonableness? The PEOs are supposed to see if the use is causing a detriment to the area. When it involves HMOs, their masters may say we need this type of housing, i.e. low-cost housing for key workers, DSS, etc, and tell them that enforcement is inappropriate or often they say the opposite and decide they do not want HMOs. My experience is that most planning enforcement officers do not understand the law and if you are polite to them, reassure them and show you are doing a good job providing decent housing, they go away. Most seem to dislike the job and do not seem to understand what they are supposed to be doing.

If the local authority decides to enforce, the property must be reverted back to what it was. If this was a pub or food takeaway, then it is better to leave as an HMO, as a pub or food takeaway causes more problems and nuisance than an HMO, i.e. enforcement of planning law is not justified. Most of what the planning officers do is a result of complaints and if you are 'nice' to the planning officer, ask their advice, listen, some will tell you what the problem is and how to get around it, especially if they think you are doing a good job in providing quality accommodation and controlling tenants. Strangely, most planning officers do not want to make someone homeless, not because many care, but because of the bad publicity that could result for the council.

However, this is not always the case and I wonder what is the motivation driving some PEOs. I appreciate that they, in practice, have very little power and it is very difficult and time-consuming for them to enforce against you. Over 99% of what they say and do is bluff. Try not to antagonise them so it gets personal and, hopefully, they will leave you alone and bully easier prey.

I am surprised by the lack of planning law knowledge of many council officials. As is so often in this business, you cannot depend on your council officials to know what they are talking about. I have had PEOs foaming at the mouth, screaming at me they know the law and they are going to make me tear down the building, only to hear nothing more from them about the matter or when we next meet.

I accept that the system is irrational and anti-HMO landlord. However, should matters get to a stage where enforcement is taken, I recommend that you always fully exploit the appeal system. Some strange decisions are made and it costs very little to appeal if you do it yourself. Though costs can be awarded, they rarely are, so I would not be intimidated by this threat. I have helped a number of landlords in what have been considered hopeless cases, yet they have won, or the council has left them alone. Appeals require a fee and are time sensitive, so you need to act quickly, but I urge you to always appeal.

Do not ignore enforcement action, this is when it becomes criminal. Appreciate that it is not criminal, a civil offence or you have done anything wrong until an enforcement notice has been made. You are perfectly safe to ignore the planners up until this stage.

Once an enforcement notice is made the position changes and you can be prosecuted if you do not comply.

Councils are now showing a greater appetite to prosecute landlords, and it gets worse. Once they have successfully prosecuted they could use the Proceeds of Crime Act against you to recover the profit made out of the rent, or even all the rent itself. A few London boroughs have done this and in one case they obtained a whopping £303K repayment order under the Proceeds of Crime Act against a landlord for failing to comply with a planning enforcement notice. Under current rules the council can keep a third of this along with all the costs of prosecuting. The rest goes to the Treasury. I suspect a number of councils are licking their lips and looking where they can do the same. Unfortunately, the government seems to be encouraging councils to prosecute landlords. (See *Dealing with Rogue Landlords* in Appendix ii.) I know a barrister who specialises in this field who is of the opinion that using the Proceeds of Crime Act against a landlord is an abuse of process. The Proceeds of Crime Act was intended to be used against serious criminals such as drug dealers. I suspect the defendants in the London cases did not robustly defend the action, so it has now set a precedent.

I would emphasise that though PEOs love to quote to you, that you can be prosecuted for not having planning permission, this is all bluff and thunder until enforcement action is officially taken.

23
Complaints to the Planning Department

This is a difficult one as most complaints are not what they seem. Yes, there may be some justification for the complaint, e.g. noise, but the birds in the morning and road traffic make a lot of noise, so why complain about this noise? Since I used Polish builders I have started to get a lot of complaints about building work. Before I could not remember getting very many complaints about building work. The real reason for the complaints is rarely the stated reason and is usually envy or more to do with racism mixed with an attitude of 'I can now get away with complaining about them'. People are much more reluctant to complain about the local builder, who may have a reputation for being a bit of a hard man, or who drinks in their local pub.

I talked to someone complaining about the Polish builders working near to where he lived. I was trying to understand what was the problem and why he had needed to complain to every council department. One of the complaints was that he did not like where they parked their vans – which was on my land, but there is a public right of way across my land. When I replied why had he not asked them to move the vans, as they would have, his reply said it all, his face screwed up in anger and contempt and he almost spat out, 'They don't speak our language, do they!'

Why did he not complain about the builders across the road who were causing more problems, e.g. noise, dust, parking, etc? I did not ask him this and I am sure if I did he would not have given me the real answer. The owner of that building site was a local nasty who would not have taken kindly to being complained about.

I would not suggest you ignore complaints, it is best to try to resolve them so as not to give the complainers justification, or at least until they can find some other reason to complain.

The usual causes of complaints to the planning or other council departments are:

I. **Fear of the unknown:** e.g. you start conversion work and one of your workers thinks it is a good joke to tell the nosy neighbour that you are going to house DSS tenants, lunatics, illegal immigrants or asylum seekers. Strictly brief your builders not to upset the neighbours. Do not let the builders know what you are doing or say you are moving in yourself.

II. **Noise:** all you need is one tenant who revs his car engine, plays his TV or radio too loud late at night, it does not even have to be a hi-fi system. I have had more problems with small radio alarm clocks being left on at full volume than I have had with hi-fi systems. I find once a neighbour focuses on noise, they often become obsessed with the property and anything becomes a cause to complain about, even the sound of the wind blowing on the property.

Try to prevent any problems and act quickly by coming down hard on the culprit causing a problem. It is better to lose a tenant than to lose your HMO business. Most of the time the inconsiderate tenants are also problem rent payers.

You find both often go together. Such tenants do not believe they should follow the rules that most people do, i.e. treat others with consideration and pay their way. You will also find that they are known to the police. Get rid of then as quickly as possible and try and avoid them in the first place.

What happens is the neighbour will complain to the council who, for reasons still not clear to me, will involve the planning department rather than the noise control section. Prevention is better than cure and it is best not to take any changes even though, since 2010 when the planning rules regarding HMOs were relaxed so planners can now do little about HMOs. It is best to avoid the aggro.

To avoid problems and keep your neighbours happy you need to be firm with prospective tenants which, as a socially responsible landlord, you should be. Let your tenant know that noise and other inconsiderate behaviour will not be tolerated and they will not be given a second chance. Nearly all my noise problems have resulted from tenants under 40 years old and mostly from those under 25. So go for an older age group and be very careful about letting to those under 40. Also be careful over letting to young couples. They are often prone to argue and/or noisy lovemaking, which disturbs the neighbours and other tenants. Couples also have a tendency to split up and then not pay their rent.

III. Parking: neighbours are often under the erroneous belief that the road outside their house is exclusively for their parking only, even if they do not have a car. Again they will complain to the council about your property, and this may be channelled to the planning department. Careful management is the solution. If parking is likely to be the problem, do not take tenants with cars. Banning them from parking in a particular area is much more difficult, as once they become a tenant you can do little to stop them apart from evicting them if they persist. You also need to try and crack down on the tenant's visitors by making it known to your tenants that they are responsible for their guests' parking.

IV. Lifestyle: the real reason for many of the complaints is lifestyle. You only have to listen carefully to what the complainers have to say and how they say it to realise that noise and parking are not the real problems. Envy, jealousy and racism are the real reasons. Why is it that this fit, able, young couple can get welfare benefits to stay at home drinking and having loud sex when we have to go to work? Foreigners coming into this country and either being kept as asylum seekers or taking our jobs! I could go on. What I find difficult to accept is that even in our so-called politically correct age that council officials will act enthusiastically on a complaint that is obviously racially motivated.

24
Resolving Planning Problems

You will often find that with a bit of bluff, and by resolving the complaining neighbours' grievances, the planning officer will stop bothering you - though it is not often that easy. Noise is a particular problem. Once a neighbour focuses on your property as causing noise then anything becomes a problem. I have had a neighbour complaining that the tenants flush the toilet at 6pm in the evening, which was the time he had his evening meal and it was putting him off his dinner.

In such circumstances, the closer you are to the C4 definition and if there is not an Article 4 Direction in place, the safer you are. Even if you are required to return the property to single occupation you will find that the planning department will give a lot of latitude, e.g. you can continue as you are, but you are not allowed to replace a tenant if they leave. The planning department do not want to appear to be the bad guys and have tenants evicted. All this will take time. If the planning department decide you are breaking planning law and the property requires planning permission, they will usually first ask you to apply for planning permission.

A planning application form is not difficult to fill in, you just need to provide a plan that you can draw yourself and pay a fee and, if you are stuck, you can always ask the planning officers to help. This is usually for free, though some authorities are now charging for advice. A planning application takes time and, of course, you will not be rushing to do it nor does the planning department move very quickly. Should your application fail, you have a right of appeal to the planning inspector. It can take months to hear appeals.

At the same time, you can make a new amended planning application and start all over again. In the meantime you are letting the property and getting rent. I had one planning appeal where I lost (unfairly) but nothing has happened and no enforcement action followed. I am still operating the HMO. All very odd.

Most of the times I have had to deal with the planning department the result has been no great conclusion. I have gone through the motions until they stopped bothering me and I am still running my HMOs. In four or ten years, all I hope will be forgiven as the planning department will be timed-barred from taking enforcement. The relaxation in planning for HMOs in 2010 also has been a lot of help.

It is not about winning battles, it is all about winning the war – stay focused on the bigger picture. If the property does not work, sell it, hopefully at a profit, and move on.

25
Why the Obscurity with Planning?

You should appreciate that there are conflicting tensions regarding HMOs. Few people like them. The government wants more housing, especially the low-cost flexible accommodation HMOs provide, but this is not necessarily the case with councils. With the lack of new house-building, HMOs are one of the few ways that the amount of accommodation in this country can be increased. Planners and many of those within councils dislike HMO landlords, especially if they seem to make a profit. Many times I have had council officials say as I am making loads of money out of my HMOs, I can easily afford the pointless expensive changes that they demand. Exploitation and profiteering are familiar words. Councils also wish to protect their housing and their role in providing housing especially to the vulnerable, and see HMO landlords as competition. They are deeply embarrassed that we can house vulnerable tenants who they are often unable to cope with a fraction of the cost they charge and are often far better at doing so.

Neighbours do not want HMOs. They do not want to have an HMO next door, especially if they house vulnerable tenants or students. The situation is not helped by HMOs being one of the few areas, along with students, motorists and dogs, that in our PC world you are allowed to discriminate against. The bigots are amongst us and I am old enough to have seen the same discrimination against immigrants, gays, disabled, single mothers, etc. Racism is still a major problem and it resurrects itself when immigrants are housed in HMOs.

The main reason for introducing an Article 4 Direction is to stop studentification happening (an area being mainly occupied by students), but the absurdity is that the student areas already exist. Article 4 Directions have only been applied to student areas, so what is the point when they are already studentified?

The result is that HMOs are treated irrationally. Few people have problems with HMOs let to professionals. It is the HMOs that are let to the unemployed and foreigners that give rise to issues. This is why, I believe, the legislators are hesitant to give the green light to HMOs, and councils impose expensive over-the-top standards. Standards are just a backdoor way to outlaw HMOs. Little in the standards stands up to any rational analysis, though these standards can, at a superficial level, appear reasonable.

Try asking questions like: "How many HMO tenants have died or have been injured by the lack of what is now being demanded?" Or, "Where is the evidence to prove that these things are wanted by HMO tenants or will benefit them?"

Ask for empirical evidence, scientific research. You will not only find any vague references as there isn't any, or the risk is no greater than with non-HMO housing.

To give only one example, I could write a book on room size. Whether a room in an HMO is 30 square feet in size or 150 square feet, there is no evidence to show that one is harmful and the other is more beneficial. An HMO tenant is free to choose what size of room they wish to pay for. Where are the tenants going to go if they are not housed in HMOs? I would argue that competition should be encouraged and let the tenants decide.

Increasingly in the cash-restricted environment in which councils have to operate, councils are seeing HMOs as a potential source of income and are looking at ways of tapping income from HMO landlords, a bit like parking control.

Councils are having to be far more entrepreneurial and introduce new sources of income to create employment for themselves. Prosecuting landlords can become an income stream because the magistrates, best known to themselves, allow the enormous fees councils allege it costs to prosecute to be recovered from the landlord in charges. HMO landlords are being treated like drug dealers and the Proceeds of Crime Act and rent repayment orders are being applied after prosecuting landlords. There is now talk of allowing councils to keep the fines, often substantial, that are awarded against landlords and the introduction of civil penalties. The law in this area is so widely drafted that a council housing officer could walk into any HMO and find something wrong and impose a fine. You can see what could and is happening.

Unfortunately landlords will not stand together and fight their councils, nor do the landlord associations show much interest in protecting their members. There is no use bitching about it. If you don't like it don't join the party. You need to know what you are doing and try and keep one step ahead.

26
Should I Buy in an Article 4 Area?

There is a school of thought that says smart investors should be buying in an area that is going to have an Article 4 Direction placed thereon. There is plenty of time to do this as it takes over a year to bring in an Article 4 Direction. The idea goes along the line that when the Article 4 comes in, rents for HMOs will rocket as there will be a shortage of HMOs in the area.

This idea has possible superficial appeal, but let's bounce it around.

Firstly, even the proposers of this idea accept that the price of properties in an Article 4 area will drop, some say by a lot. Article 4 areas usually have a high existing HMO population and if HMO landlords are not buying, and owner-occupiers are not going to buy as they will not want to live in areas with a high density of HMOs, who will buy? Well, for a start, if the price drops enough, how about landlords who single-let?

The problem with this view is that it is untested, subjective, and based on no evidence whatsoever. My experience of property is that it is rarely logical and areas vary. Yes, property prices have dropped in areas of Belfast where Article 4 has been introduced, but Northern Ireland has very different problems regarding property to the mainland and most property in Northern Ireland has substantially dropped in value and rents are stagnant. However, my main issue is: what landlord is going to buy a property when they know the value is going to drop or at the very least be uncertain? Will the approach of 'buy for income, never mind the loss of property capital value' ever take off?

I have heard some say that the introduction of an Article 4 Direction will create ghettos where properties will become un-mortgageable and values will collapse. In some of the proposed Article 4 student areas, there has already been a substantial drop in demand due to the reduction of student numbers and the building of student villages/flats by commercial investors. Will the introduction of Article 4 do anything to help? I doubt it.

Secondly, will rent levels rocket? Most Article 4 areas tend to be fairly small and a significant differential in rent levels may develop if rent in the Article 4 area increases to any great amount (HMO tenants, generally only rent an HMO as they cannot afford a flat or house) . I don't know and I doubt anyone knows. As I have said before, the property market is not logical.

I remember discussing in 2004, new city centre flats in Birmingham selling for £70K when less than two miles down the road you could buy an old terraced house in a grotty street with a large garden for £30K. I wondered why anyone would entertain a leasehold flat with service charges in the thousands at such a price. Three years later, I was totally bemused to find these flats were selling for over £200K and prices were rising, and the terraced houses were only fetching £90K. Will you get the same thing happening with HMO rents? I will not be taking the risk myself, though I do believe it may be easier to rent HMOs in those areas, and so you could be more selective as to the type of tenant you take. But again I have no evidence to support this.

Finally, will an Article 4 directive make any difference? The feedback I have had about Article 4 areas and I should add I have not done any extensive research, is that landlords are ignoring Article 4 directives and are multi-letting without planning permission, and local authorities are not enforcing. That it will put off cautious landlords from buying and lenders from lending in these area is undeniable.

The HMO landlords I grew up with before the 2010 relaxation, which allowed small HMOs of up to six tenants to be set up as HMOs with little regard to the planners, (mostly student landlords) would say that student lets were within the existing law and many local authorities did not even consider students lets an HMO. When profit and the fine points of the law clash, the law always suffers and I believe the same will happen again. HMO landlords will ignore the Article 4 direction. Those pre-2010 landlords will say their local authorities knew about them and, as they did nothing to stop them, they must not have been doing anything wrong. If it is not enforced it does not exist. Unfortunately, that is not always the case, but if you can get away with it, so what? No crime is being committed.

If you operate an HMO in an Article 4 area without planning permission the planners, after lengthy action, can stop you by serving an enforcement order, which you can appeal against. In other words, the worst that can happen is that you must stop letting it as an HMO, there is no fine, penalty or other sanctions, unless you are stupid enough to break an enforcement order.

With the enormous cutbacks on local authorities' spending, will many local authorities have the resources to maintain their own properties or take any interest in HMOs?

The other view is that enforcement may increase as local authorities will see enforcement as a way to justify jobs. As for creating income, planning applications for an HMO are free in an Article 4 area so this is going to be a cost, but there is a possibility that enforcement, if it leads to prosecution, could produce income as the cost of prosecution can be recovered and if rent payment order under the proceedings of Crime Act is given, the local authority gets a share of this. A bit like if the police sneakily set traps to catch you, instead of warning you they are going to prosecute or fine you if they catch you speeding, parking, etc.

In conclusion, as with so much in this business, there is a change in name and things go on much as they have always done. I would not invest in an area just because it was going to get an Article 4 designation. I would invest in an area because I was confident it would work. It would also be nice if I liked the areas, but this is not always possible.

If you already own a property in a proposed Article 4 area it may be to your advantage to consider turning it into a small

HMO, or then again you might be better to sell while you can. It is times like this when the wise are fearful that the brave (reckless) investor can make enormous profit or loss.

Best of luck.

Appendix i

Department for Communities and Local Government

Communities and Local Government Circular 08/2010

Department for Communities and Local Government

Eland House, Bressenden Place, London SWIE 5DU

November 2010

CHANGES TO PLANNING REGULATIONS FOR DWELLING HOUSES AND HOUSES IN MULTIPLE OCCUPATION

INTRODUCTION

1. This circular gives guidance on planning regulations, in particular on changes of use for dwelling houses and houses in multiple occupation following changes to legislation in April and October 2010. The general effect of these changes is to allow changes of use between dwelling houses and houses in multiple occupation to take place without the need for an application for planning permission, unless a local authority has specifically identified an area in which planning applications will be required.

2. A high concentration of shared homes can sometimes cause problems, especially if too many properties in one area are let to short-term tenants with little stake in the local community. So changes to legislation will give councils the freedom to choose areas where landlords must submit a

planning application to rent their properties to unrelated tenants (i.e. houses in multiple occupation). This will enable high concentrations of houses in multiple occupation to be controlled where local authorities decide there is a problem, but will prevent landlords across the country being driven from the rental market by high costs and red tape.

3. The circular gives general guidance only. To be certain that changes of use in specific cases are lawful and do not require planning permission, advice should be sought from the local planning authority or other sources of professional advice. In particular, in certain circumstances local planning authorities are able to issue directions that require applications for planning permission to be submitted where they would not normally be needed – see paragraph 14 below.

4. The guidance replaces guidance set out in circular 05/2010[1], and the guidance in paragraphs 66-77 of the circular 03/2005[2].

BACKGROUND

5. Under Planning Legislation[3], the requirement to obtain planning permission covers not only new building work but also changes in use of buildings or land.

6. However, the Use Classes Order[4] places uses of land and buildings into various classes. Changes of use within a class do not require an application for planning permission. In addition, there are also separate provisions that allow

changes of use between certain classes in the Order without the need for planning permission. These are set out in separate legislation – the General Permitted Development Order[5] – and are known as permitted development rights.

7. Dwelling houses and small houses in multiple occupation are now covered by the following classes in the Use Classes Order:

Class C3: Dwelling houses – this class is formed of 3 parts:

- C3(a): those living together as a single household as defined by the Housing Act 2004 (basically a 'family');
- C3(b): those living together as a single household and receiving care, and
- C3(c): those living together as a single household who do not fall within the C4 definition of a house in multiple occupation.

Class C4: Houses in multiple occupation (3-6 occupants) – in broad terms, the new C4 class covers small shared houses or flats occupied by between 3 and 6 unrelated individuals who share basic amenities.

Large houses in multiple occupation (those with more than 6 people sharing) – these are unclassified by the Use Classes Order. In planning terms they are described as being sui generis (of their own kind). In consequence, a planning application will be required for a change of use from a dwelling house to a large house in multiple occupation or from a Class C4 house in multiple occupation to a large house in multiple occupation where a material change of use is considered to have taken place. Paragraph 17 of Annex A to this circular provides further guidance on this.

8. Detailed guidance on the classes in the Use Classes Order which cover dwelling houses and houses in multiple occupation is set out in Annex A to this circular.

I. Communities and Local Government Circular 05/2010 Changes to planning regulations for dwelling houses and houses in multiple occupation (March 2010)
II. See ODPM Circular 03/2005 Changes of use of buildings and land (March 2005).
III. The Town and Country Planning Act 1990 4   The Town and Country Planning (Use Classes) Order 1987 (as amended) 5   The Town and Country Planning (General Permitted Development) Order 1995 (as amended)

AMENDMENTS TO LEGISLATION MADE IN 2010

9. On 6 April 2010, an amendment to the Use Classes Order[6] introduced a definition of small-scale houses in multiple occupation into the planning system. It effectively split the old Class C3 (dwelling houses) class into 2 separate classes – Class C3 (dwelling houses) and Class C4 (houses in multiple occupation).

10. The result of this was that development previously falling under Class C3 was reclassified and now falls into

either the new C3 or C4 Classes. This reclassification does not amount to a change of use under planning legislation (it is not classified as development) – so no consequences arise from the reclassification in terms of the need to seek planning permission.

11. A further amendment was also made in April 2010 to the General Permitted Development Order[7]. This gave permitted development rights for changes of use from C4 to C3, thereby allowing a change of use from a small-scale house in multiple occupation to a dwelling house without the need to apply for planning permission.

12. The amendment to the General Permitted Development Order also restated class C2A (secure residential accommodation) for clarity, as some opinions had been expressed that this class applied only to the Crown, when that was not the intention. Guidance on Class C2A is also included in Annex B to this circular.

13. On 1 October 2010 further amendments were made to the General Permitted Development Order[8]. These changes gave permitted development rights for changes of use from C3 to C4.

14. The April and October changes to legislation mean that from 1 October 2010 a change of use from a dwelling house (class C3) to a house in multiple occupation (Class C4) and from a house in multiple occupation to a dwelling house is possible under permitted development rights and planning applications are not needed.

15. However, as with most types of permitted development rights, local authorities will be able to use existing powers, in the form of article 4 directions, to remove these rights and require planning applications for such changes of use in defined areas. Anyone considering a change of use from a dwelling house to a house in multiple occupation or vice versa is advised to contact the local planning authority for the area concerned to check whether any article 4 directions have been made.

16. In addition to the amendments to the Use Classes Order and the General Permitted Development Order, new regulations[9] reduced local authorities' liability to pay compensation where they choose to make article 4 directions to remove permitted development rights in relation to houses in multiple occupation. As a result:

The Town and Country Planning (Use Classes) (Amendment) (England) Order 2010 (SI 2010/653) 7 The Town and Country Planning (General Permitted Development) (Amendment) (England) Order 2010 (SI 2010/654) 8 The Town and Country Planning (General Permitted Development) (Amendment) (No.2) (England) Order 2010 (SI 2010/2134) 9 The Town and Country Planning (Compensation) (No.3) (England) Regulations 2010 (SI 2010/2135)

 i. where a local authority gives 12 months' advance notice of a direction taking effect there will be no liability to pay compensation
 ii. where directions are made with immediate effect or less than 12 months' notice, compensation will only

be payable in relation to planning applications which are submitted within 12 months of the effective date of the direction and which are then either refused or granted subject to conditions.

Cancellation of guidance

Department for Communities and Local Government circular 05/2010, and paragraphs 66-77 of the Office of the Deputy Prime Minister circular 03/2005 are hereby cancelled.

Annex A

DWELLING HOUSES AND HOUSES IN MULTIPLE OCCUPATION – GUIDANCE ON CLASSES Class C3 (dwelling houses)

1. This class is now formed of three parts:

- C3(a): those living together as a single household as defined by the Housing Act 2004 (basically a 'family')
- C3(b): those living together as a single household and receiving care, and
- C3(c): those living together as a single household who do not fall within the C4 definition of a house in multiple occupation.

For the purposes of C3(b) and (c) single household is not defined in the legislation.

2. There is no limit on the number of members of the single household under C3(a). The limit for C3(b) and (c) is no more than six people.

3. A single household under C3(a) is formed by a family (a couple whether married or not with members of the family of one of the couple to be treated as members of the family of the other), an employer and certain domestic employees (such as an au pair, nanny, nurse, governess, servant, chauffeur, gardener, secretary and personal assistant), a carer and the person receiving the care and a foster parent and foster child.

4. C3(b) continues to make provision for supported housing schemes, such as those for people with disabilities or mental health problems.

5. It remains the case that in small residential care homes or nursing homes, staff and residents will probably not live as a single household and the use will therefore fall into the residential institutions class (Class C2), regardless of the size of the home. Local planning authorities should include any resident care staff in their calculation of the number of people accommodated.

6. C3(c) allows for groups of people (up to six) living together as a single household. This is to allow for those groupings that do not fall within the C4 house in multiple occupation definition to be provided for e.g. a small religious community may fall into this section as could a homeowner who is living with a lodger.

7. The term 'dwelling house' is not defined in this part of the Use Classes Order. The question of whether a particular building is a dwelling house will therefore depend on the facts of that case.

8. The common feature of all premises which can be generally be described as dwelling houses is that they are buildings that ordinarily afford the facilities required for day to day private domestic existence. It is recognised that unlikely or unusual buildings, such as churches or windmills, have been used as, or adapted to become, dwelling houses. Whilst such premises may not be regarded as dwelling

houses in the traditional sense, they may be so classified for the purposes of the Use Classes Order.

9. The criteria for determining whether the use of particular premises should be classified within the C3 use class include both the manner of the use and the physical condition of the premises. Premises can properly be regarded as being used as a single dwelling house where they are:

- a single, self-contained unit of occupation which can be regarded as being a separate 'planning unit' distinct from any other part of the building containing them;
- designed or adapted for residential purposes-containing the normal facilities for cooking, eating and sleeping associated with use as a dwelling house;

This would not include bed-sitting rooms. Here the planning unit is likely to be the whole building which would therefore be classified as a house in multiple occupation.

Class C4: Houses in multiple occupation (3-6 occupants)

10. In broad terms, the new C4 class covers small shared houses or flats occupied by between three and six unrelated individuals who share basic amenities.

11. Small bed-sits will be classified as C4.

12. To fall within the 'house in multiple occupation' definition, a property must be occupied as the main residence. Guests visiting for short periods should not be included in any calculation of number of occupants.

Students, migrants and asylum seekers who do not occupy the property all year will be considered as occupying the property as their main residence and should be included in any calculation of occupant numbers.

13. Social housing is excluded from C4 as are care homes, children's homes and bail hostels. Properties occupied by students which are managed by the education establishment, those occupied for the purposes of a religious community whose main occupation is prayer, contemplation, education and the relief of the suffering are also excluded. Some of these uses will be in C3, others will be in other use classes or fall to be treated as sui generis.

14. Properties containing the owner and up to two lodgers do not constitute a house in multiple occupation for these purposes.

15. To classify as a house in multiple occupation a property does not need to be converted or adapted in any way.

Large houses in multiple occupation

16. Large houses in multiple occupation – those with more than six people sharing – are unclassified by the Use Classes order and are therefore considered to be 'sui generis'.

17. Although the control limit of six persons defines the scope of the C3 (b) and (c) dwelling houses and C4 houses in multiple occupation classes, this does not imply that any excess of that number must constitute a breach of planning control. A material change of use will occur only where the

total number of residents has increased to the point where it can be said that the use has intensified so as to become of a different character or the residents in relation to C3 no longer constitute a single household.

Annex B

GUIDANCE ON CLASS C2A AND CLASS D1

Class C2A: Secure residential institutions

1. Class C2A is for secure residential institutions, which enables changes between similar types of premises (but with different uses) to be made without requiring planning permission for a change of use.

2. The list of institutions falling within the C2A class is not exhaustive. The list contains two types of institution:

a) those uses covering where security is concerned with preventing the residents from leaving. This will include all the various categories of secure facilities in the criminal justice and immigration estates, as well as secure local authority accommodation and secure hospitals (these share the land use characteristics and impacts of some of the Crown uses).
b) uses such as military barracks, where security is concerned with preventing unauthorised entry, but where the planning impacts are similar to some of the other uses identified in (a) above. For example, it might be possible to convert a disused military barracks to a low-category prison without major perimeter works.

3. A new C2A development such as a prison, secure hospital or immigration detention centre will require a planning application. These types of development require a large area of ground. Such uses need good road links for staff, visitors

and deliveries and space for car-parking as well as good public transport links. They also provide a significant number of long-term jobs for local people. For these reasons such institutions may not easily be accommodated within existing residential land allocations. The Secretary of State considers that the physical requirements and employment-generating aspects of these schemes are an important consideration and that despite their residential classification, location on land allocated for employment uses is appropriate.

Class D1: Non-residential institutions

4. Class D1 (non-residential institutions) also includes use as a law court. Law courts have similar planning impacts to other D1 uses, such as art galleries, museums and exhibition halls, where people come and go throughout the day.

Published by TSO (The Stationery Office) and available from:

Online: www.tsoshop.c.uk

Mail: PO Box 29, Norwich, NR3 1GN

Telephone orders/General enquiries: 0870 600 5522

Fax orders: 0870 600 5533

E-mail: customer.services@tso.co.uk

Textphone: 0870 240 3701

TSO@Blackwell and other Accredited Agents

Customers can also order publications from:

TSO Ireland, 16 Arthur Street, Belfast, BT1 4GD

Tel: 028 9023 8451

Fax: 028 9023 5401

© Crown copyright 2010

Copyright in the typographical arrangements rests with the Crown.

Published for the Department for Communities and Local Government, under licence from the Controller of Her Majesty's Stationery Office.

Extracts of up to 10 per cent of this publication may be

photocopied for non-commercial in-house use, subject to the source being acknowledged.

Application for reproduction should be made in writing to:

Office of Public Sector Information, Information Policy Team, Kew, Richmond, Surrey TW9 4DU.

Printed by The Stationery Office Ltd under the authority and superintendence of the Controller of Her Majesty's Stationery Office and Queen's Printer of Acts of Parliament. ISBN 978 0 11 754104 7

Appendix ii

Dealing with Rogue Landlords

A Guide for Local Authorities

August 2012 Department for Communities and Local Government

© Crown copyright, 2012

Copyright in the typographical arrangement rests with the Crown.

You may re-use this information (not including logos) free of charge in any format or medium, under the terms of the Open Government Licence. To view this licence, visit http://www.nationalarchives.gov.uk/doc/open-government-licence/ or write to the Information Policy Team, The National Archives, Kew, London TW9 4DU, or e-mail: psi@nationalarchives.gsi.gov.uk.

This document/publication is also available on our website at www.communities.gov.uk

Any enquiries regarding this document/publication should be sent to us at:

Department for Communities and Local Government
Eland House
Bressenden Place
London
SW1E 5DU

Telephone: 030 3444 0000

August, 2012

ISBN: 978-1-4098- 3623-0

CONTENTS

Foreword by the Housing Minister, Grant Shapps MP and the Immigration Minister Damian Green MP

Introduction

Rogue Landlords – Diagnosing the Problem

Rogue Landlords – Taking Action

Rogue Landlords – Prosecution and Deterring Criminality

Conclusion

Further Information

Annex A – Local Authority Powers

Annex B – Powers of Other Agencies

A Joint Foreword by the Housing Minister Grant Shapps MP and the Immigration Minister Damian Green MP

When it comes to housing, this Government is committed to providing choice and opportunity for all. The demand for rented homes is high and the private rented sector has grown rapidly in recent years with around 3.6 million households – 17% of all – in England now renting their home from a private landlord. We want to help the private rented sector to grow and meet the continuing demand for good quality rented housing.

Overall the sector is performing well. However a small minority of landlords fail to meet their basic responsibilities and in some cases act in a way which is outright criminal. These rogue landlords often target vulnerable people, placing them in overcrowded or poor quality accommodation. In some places people are living in squalid outbuildings or makeshift accommodation – beds in sheds.

The false promises of work and accommodation are the key means by which illegal migrants are tempted to the UK and then exploited. The activities of rogue landlords helps fuel illegal working and benefit fraud and the harmful effects of their activities go beyond those individuals whom they exploit. The victims of crime are also the wider community and those whose local services are robbed of resources. Allowing the development of a "shadow" housing market carries wider dangers to public health and community relations.

This is simply unacceptable in modern Britain, and we have been working across Whitehall and with overseas Governments to tackle the problem. We have also been working with local authorities to discover the extent of the problem and the barriers that they face in tackling rogue landlords. We have awarded £1.8m to the nine local authorities who have the biggest problem with beds in sheds.

From this partnership we have produced this good practice guidance, to share experience and knowledge with all local authorities so that they can effectively tackle rogue landlords. By working together we can stamp out rogue landlords and eliminate unacceptable housing in the sector.

Rt Hon Grant Shapps MP
Minister for Housing

Damian Green MP
Minister for Immigration

Introduction

I. Local authorities have highlighted a significant and growing problem with rogue landlords. These landlords target vulnerable tenants and place them in overcrowded or poorly maintained accommodation. In some places there has been an increase in the use of outbuildings as living accommodation. As well as the impact on tenants, these poor living conditions can have a huge impact on neighbourhoods leading to problems with excessive waste, sewage and in some cases an increase in crime and anti-social behaviour. In some places, rogue landlords have specifically targeted migrants, some of whom are in the UK illegally. This can lead to serious problems in a neighbourhood including illegal working, benefit fraud and tensions between communities.

II. Local authorities should take swift and decisive action to tackle rogue landlords. It is important that local authorities take leadership on this issue and prioritise action as tackling rogue landlords can have improve the quality of life for a whole community.

III. Local authorities should:
- Understand the nature and extent of the problems in their area;
- Take swift and decisive action to stop rogue landlords using unsuitable accommodation to house tenants;
- Prosecute rogue landlords and deter others by building effective cases and publicising successful

IV. prosecutions. This guidance provides practical advice on how local authorities can step up their work to tackle rogue landlords drawing on the experience of local authorities already working on these issues.

1. Rogue Landlords: Diagnosing the Problem

I. It can be difficult to establish the extent and nature of the problems caused by rogue or criminal landlords. Problems can be highly localised and well hidden. Many local authorities rely on concerns being raised by tenants or neighbours. However, vulnerable tenants can be afraid to raise issues with the local authority or unaware of their rights. Staff working on planning enforcement and on licensing Houses of Multiple Occupation will have the best intelligence about the housing stock in their area and about landlords operating locally. It is important that local authorities work proactively to identify problems by:

- Sharing intelligence across the authority to identify hotspots. In many authorities, problems are concentrated in small areas, sometimes individual streets. Teams working on investigating complaints, planning enforcement and licensing of Houses in Multiple Occupation will all have intelligence to share on hotspots and sometimes on particular landlords in the area.
- Cross-referencing data the local authority holds. Some authorities have cross-referenced their Housing Benefit

database with properties licensed as Houses in Multiple Occupation. If a property is licensed for four occupants but there are six claimants at the address, the authority knows to investigate. Similarly, Council Tax data can sometimes highlight where outbuildings are being used illegally as dwellings. The case study gives more information about how Housing Benefit information can be used to detect landlord criminality.

- Clear policies and processes for dealing with complaints from residents/tenants. This means effective triaging of complaints so cases can be prioritised; documented procedures to ensure processes are thoroughly and consistently applied and clarity about which teams should be involved at each stage. Many local authorities have set out clear process maps so that colleagues have a step by step process to follow.

II. If you suspect that there is a problem in an area, it is important to quantify and understand it. Local authorities may consider –

- Targeted investigation of areas including door to door surveys. The London Borough of Ealing has undertaken a road to road inspection of parts of their Borough using a multidisciplinary team to identify possible rogue landlords.
- Working with other agencies. Section 2 of this guidance deals with working with other agencies to tackle rogue landlords and the advantages that working together can provide.

Bury Case Study – Working across the authority to tackle rogue landlords

A Channel 4 *Dispatches* programme identified significant issues with properties owned by the Meridian Foundation. The local authority followed this up with joint action from two of their departments, Urban Renewal and the Benefits Service.

The aim of Benefits Service was to assess why housing benefit was being paid direct to the landlord in 39 out of the 46 cases. They speculated that:

- Meridian were deliberately targeting vulnerable tenants (creating contrived tenancies)
- Meridian were misrepresenting the fact that their tenants were vulnerable
- Benefit fraud may have been taking place

The Urban Renewal unit were involved to tackle housing standards issues.

How and using what powers?

Unannounced visits were led by staff from the Benefits Service supported by environmental health officers. This approach negated the need for the potential use of powers of entry by Urban Renewal. Urban Renewal staff inspected properties using the Housing Health and Safety Rating System, under the Housing Act 2004. 46 properties (identified from existing council records) were visited.

Results

- Category 1 hazards were found in 14 properties.
- The landlord agreed to address the hazards and an Environmental Health Officer is overseeing this process.
- Some Housing Benefit claims have been cancelled where there has been no response to the request for contact by the Benefits Service.
- Several customers are no longer classed as vulnerable.
- Only 18 housing benefit claims are now being paid direct to the landlord, down from 39.

2. Rogue Landlords – Taking Action

Local Authority Powers

I. The problem of rogue landlords varies considerably from area to area. In some areas, homes may be poorly maintained and dangerously overcrowded. In others, landlords are renting outbuildings as permanent living accommodation compromising the safety of their tenants and causing significant problems for neighbours. Some local authorities have also discovered that vacant commercial premises, often in poor repair, are being used as living accommodation. Local authorities should take action in all these circumstances.

II. If local authorities have concerns about the quality of the accommodation provided in any residential property then they should take action under the Housing Act 2004. The Housing Health and Safety Rating System is used to assess housing conditions in all residential property. Local authorities have a duty to take enforcement action to secure necessary improvements where Category 1 (serious) hazards are present, and the discretion to intervene where Category 2 hazards are present. Annex A provides more details of these powers and the enforcement action which can be taken if hazards are found.

III. Some home-owners choose to build annexes to their property for legitimate reasons, following planning law and applying for permissions where necessary. However, where outbuildings are being used as separate residential accommodation without planning permission this is likely to be a breach of planning control and local authorities should take action. Even where there are no hazards within these properties, they may create problems in the wider neighbourhood (for example, with sewage and drainage, or noise). Ultimately a local authority can issue a planning enforcement notice which may prohibit a building's use and in some circumstances require demolition.

IV. Local authorities can use both housing and planning powers simultaneously to take action against rogue landlords. Where using the powers together it is important that they do not conflict. Some local authorities have found it more effective to issue planning notices first followed by Prohibition or Demolition Orders under the Housing Act. Annex A to this guidance document sets out the full range of powers at a local authority's disposal when considering how to deal with rogue landlords.

V. Local authorities have the powers to enter land for obtaining the information required for housing and planning enforcement purposes at any reasonable hour and can enter any building used as a dwelling house giving 24 hours notice. If entry is refused or the local authority believes that a case is urgent they can obtain a warrant to enter from a Justice of the Peace. This system strikes a balance between protecting civil liberties and enabling local authorities to take enforcement action.

VI. The two case studies below demonstrate different approaches taken in different circumstances. In Southwark, the authority used the Housing Act 2004 to prohibit use of a property which was overcrowded and unfit for tenants. In Brent, the authority required that an outhouse was demolished as it had contravened planning law by being used as a dwelling.

Case Study Southwark
Emergency Prohibition Order

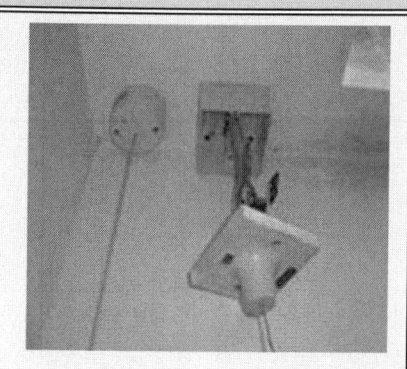

The Property:
The property was a first floor five room flat above a cafe. The room occupied by the complainant was approximately nine square metres in area and was occupied by two adults and two children (a boy and girl aged two and seven). The other room was smaller and was occupied by four adults using a set of single bunk beds. The local authority understood that the other three rooms were occupied by up to four people.

Hazards:
All facilities were in an extremely poor state of repair. The

only cooking facilities were located at the top of the stairs which led to the flat. The cooker was located on the means of escape from fire. If there was a fire caused by cooking or an electrical fault (the most common cause of a fire in Houses in Multiple Occupation) the escape route would be blocked and the occupants trapped in the building. There was no fire protection in the flat.

Action:
- An emergency prohibition order was served prohibiting the use of the flat as residential accommodation.
- The family was supported by Social Services.
- The other occupants received letters advising them to seek advice about their situation.

Case Study: Brent – Planning Enforcement of Outbuildings

Brent Council first became aware of a large outhouse being constructed in the garden of a residential premises in September 2007. Builders claimed they were building a garage. After an investigation, the Council served a planning contravention notice but no reply was received to it

In January 2009, Brent Council carried out a further inspection of the premises and building work had been completed. It took some time to gain access but by then it was clear that the premises were a self-contained flat. Following that visit the Council sent letters of warning and then issued an enforcement notice requiring the demolition of the building. An appeal was lodged and dismissed by September 2010 and the building was vacated but not demolished by the compliance deadline.

Council officers therefore visited the building and demolished it. Demolishing it meant the Council was assured that it could not be reused at a later date.

See photographs of the premises below:

Before demolition:

After demolition:

VII. In some areas, rogue landlords focus their activities on Houses in Multiple Occupation. If local authorities are concerned about the management or condition of Houses in Multiple Occupation in their area they can consider Additional Houses in Multiple Occupation Licensing Schemes. If the authority has wider concerns about privately rented housing in their area, they can consider selective licensing schemes. Selective licensing is a discretionary power allowing local authorities to license all privately rented properties in a specific area that suffers either from low housing demand or from significant and persistent antisocial behaviour. Annex A sets out more detail on how local authorities can operate these licensing schemes.

VIII. If local authorities are concerned about the construction of outbuildings in a neighbourhood with an acute local problem, they can make an Article 4 Direction to withdraw 'permitted development' rights under certain circumstances. An Article 4 Direction would not prevent the construction of an outbuilding on a property, but instead require that planning permission was first obtained from the local authority. While this would not remove the need for proactive enforcement activity, it would help authorities gain more control over future development.

Preventing Homelessness

IX. Local authorities will also want to consider the impact of their action on tenants, and share information with homelessness services particularly where enforcement action is planned.

X. In some cases those accommodated may be migrants, some here illegally. Many will have no recourse to public funds. Local authorities should report anyone they suspect to be in the UK illegally to the UK Border Agency. Local authorities should also consider reconnecting migrants to their home country especially where the alternative is for them to become destitute and sleep rough. Authorities may also wish to consider the provision of short-term accommodation ("reconnection beds") where people have volunteered to return home to prevent rough sleeping.

XI. Local authorities will want to work closely with voluntary sector partners to ensure that anyone displaced from beds in sheds or other unsuitable accommodation is picked up and does not end up rough sleeping. Local authorities should work closely with the UK Border Agency who will be able to confirm which individuals have illegal immigration status and take action. Where Accession 10 nationals are involved the UK Border Agency should also be involved in case administrative removal is being considered for those not exercising their Treaty Rights.

Working with other Agencies

XII. In some cases, landlord criminality will be linked to other issues, such as providing illegal employment, benefit fraud, or tax evasion. In some parts of the country, outbuildings are occupied by predominantly migrant workers, some of which may be in the UK illegally. Local authorities will need to combine forces with other agencies – and may wish to form focussed multi-disciplinary teams.

The UK Border Agency

XIII. The UK Border Agency is an operational agency of the Home Office and is responsible for controlling immigration and enforcing related rules. It considers applications for permission to enter or stay in the UK, citizenship and asylum applications and will seek to deport those foreign nationals who commit criminal offences and to administratively remove those who have committed offences under immigration legislation such as entering the UK illegally, overstaying permission to stay or gaining permission to stay in the UK by deception. The Agency works alongside the new

Border Force which is a separate operational command within the Home Office and is responsible for the protection of the United Kingdom's border.

XIV. The UK Border Agency's enforcement function is structured around Local Immigration Teams who work with the public and alongside police, HM Revenue & Customs, local authorities and other local partners. They are able to offer advice and support in determining a person's immigration status and whether they may have committed an immigration offence. Each Local Immigration Team has a leader who is the local point of contact for any UK Border Agency enquiry during office hours. The team works with the community and develops the local knowledge needed to tackle the area's specific needs, and to understand and address the local impact of migration. Local authorities should be aware of their Local Immigration Team contact and should seek to involve them in any enforcement activity where they suspect illegal immigrants are involved. More on the powers held by UK Border Agency officers can be found at Annex B.

Police

XV. Where a local authority suspects that more widespread criminal activity may be associated with landlord criminality, it is appropriate to involve the Police. The Police have considerable powers of search and arrest without warrant where circumstances permit. These include the power to arrest without warrant persons suspected of committing criminal offences relating to immigration, such as assisting unlawful immigration. They also have the power to arrest for a number of other potentially relevant offences including conspiracy to defraud, fraud, forgery and counterfeiting, trafficking for sexual exploitation, possessing and making false identity documents. They also have the power to enter and search without warrant premises owned or occupied by someone arrested for an immigration offence to search for nationality documents, or enter other premises under warrant to apprehend suspected immigration offenders.

XVI. The Police can assist local authorities in conducting joint visits to premises as part of a locally agreed partnership plan to reduce Anti Social Behaviour and crime associated with landlord criminality and/or beds in sheds. This can assist build the local problem profile by gathering and sharing data in relation to premises, occupants and landlords. This in turn will help inform decision-making, risk management and prioritizing activity to tackle associated crime and Anti Social Behaviour. In Ealing for example the local authority has established a multi-disciplinary team including a funded police officer to develop a problem profile, joint intelligence product, and enforcement tactics using Proceeds of Crime Act legislation. Similar arrangements have developed between Local Authorities and the Police to tackle a range of locally agreed priorities such as Anti Social Behaviour. Other practice is developing between Local authorities and partners such as the Police, the UK Border Agency, and Fire and Rescue Services in conducting visits to tackle related issues.

The Fire and Rescue Service

XVII. Fire and rescue authorities and local authorities are expected to work closely together to ensure risks to their communities are identified and effectively mitigated. Fire and rescue authorities consider on the basis of individual cases whether the Regulatory Reform (Fire Safety) Order 2005 applies to the premises and the extent to which they have power of entry (without use of force) to domestic premises for the purposes of inspection and enforcement of general fire safety. Generally, premises exclusively occupied as a single private dwelling (including the garden, outbuildings, sheds etc.) are outside the scope of the Fire Safety Order. However, the common parts of multi-occupied residential premises, such as Houses in Multiple Occupation or blocks of flats are subject to the general fire safety requirements of the Fire Safety Order. In addition, the emergency powers of fire and rescue authorities to prohibit or restrict the use of premises in cases of risk of death or serious injury from fire (including power of entry to inspect) are extended under the Fire Safety Order and apply to domestic premises that are not premises consisting of or comprised in a house which is occupied as a single private dwelling. This includes flats and bedsits in blocks or Houses in Multiple Occupation and other premises that cannot reasonably be construed as a 'house' that is occupied as a single dwelling. Local authorities and fire and rescue authorities should work together to ensure the safety of domestic premises including providing fire safety advice to households (such as the benefits of a working smoke alarm).

Her Majesty's Revenue and Customs

XVIII. Where Local Authorities have a suspicion that a landlord has not declared rental income they can disclose that information to HM Revenue and Customs. Section 29 of the Data Protection Act 1998 provides a specific exemption for disclosure to HM Revenue and Customs for the purposes of the assessment or collection of tax. Penalties for tax evasion can be large – up to 100% of the tax due – and can act as a significant deterrent. Illegal activity by rogue landlords can go beyond their rental income and they can be involved in the wider illegal economy. It is therefore very important that local authorities involve HM Revenue and Customs if they have any suspicion of landlord involvement in the illegal economy.

3. Rogue Landlords – Prosecution and Deterring Criminality

Prosecution:

I. Local authorities must consider carefully before bringing prosecutions, but where a landlord persists in illegally letting property, local authorities should prosecute through the Courts. Different penalties apply depending on the nature of the offence and the enforcement route authorities have used to tackle the issue. These are set out at Annex A to this guidance. In preparing an effective case for prosecution, local authorities should:

- Act promptly in bringing cases to Court. While local authorities will wish to work with landlords to try to reach a solution without prosecution, once this has proved unsuccessful, local authorities should act swiftly in bringing the case against a landlord to Court.
- Invest in good legal advocacy and training for staff. Planning enforcement teams and private housing officers should be trained on how to gather and give evidence. A strong management commitment will be needed to engage and resource legal teams especially when dealing with the Proceeds of Crime Act, Rent Repayment Orders, other Residential Property Tribunal appeals and licensing matters.
- Gather and present as much evidence as possible about the nature of the breach or hazard. Keeping thorough records of how the local authority has dealt with the enforcement action will be helpful in bringing successful

prosecutions and local authorities should present impact statements as part of their cases to give a sense of the impact the landlord's actions have had on their tenants and the wider community.

- Bring joint prosecutions. Where breaches of both housing and planning legislation are occurring at a property, enforcement officers should consider combining the charges in one Court action to ensure that Magistrates appreciate the overall picture and issue costs and fines accordingly.

2. Even where a prosecution is successful, the fines issued to landlords found guilty of offences can vary hugely. The maximum fine that landlords can receive for failing to comply with a prohibition order or other statutory notice issued by the local authority will be unlimited when the recently passed Legal Aid, Sentencing and Punishment of Offenders Act comes into force later this year. However, magistrates take into consideration the financial circumstances of the offender when determining the level of fine they set. In practice, if a landlord's income is low or they do not declare their full earnings this can mean they face a low level of fine for these offences. To combat this, local authorities should, where possible, provide any evidence they have available of the landlord's earnings from the property or properties concerned. This may help magistrates determine an appropriate level of fine for the offence.

3. Local authorities should also consider using the Proceeds

of Crime Act and seeking Rent Repayment Orders after prosecuting landlords. If a defendant has been convicted of a listed serious offence or has a history of a number of convictions, the court can assume that all their property is the proceeds of crime and this can be factored into the amount of a confiscation order. Separately, under the Housing Act 2004, the local authority may recover rents paid as Housing Benefit where a licensable property has not been licensed. Further information on the Proceeds of Crime Act can be found at Annex A but some local authorities have already used this successfully in cases of landlord criminality. An example of the sums that can be levied against landlords and received by the local authority from successful use of the Proceeds of Crime Act and Rent Repayment Orders are below.

Example of Proceeds of Crime Act Prosecutions (London Borough of Newham):

Address	Confiscation Order awarded by the courts	Council Share @ 37%	Total Costs to the Council including legal costs
Property 1	£22,218.50	£8,220.80	£4,500
Property 2	£62,149.34	£22,995.20	£8,000
Property 3	£12,005	£4,441.85	£6,500
Property 4	£8,240	£3,048.80	£11,000
Total	£104,612.84	£38,706.65	£30,000

Example of Rent Repayment Order recovery data (London Borough of Newham):

Address	Rent Repayment Order sought	Rent Repayment Order granted by RPTS	Total Costs (inc legal costs)
Total (2)	£10,432.60	£10,432.60	£7,371.68

4. Local authorities should also consider working together to prosecute landlords. This can result in much higher fines as Magistrates have the full picture of the scope and extent of a landlord's activities. The case study below sets out a successful example of a joint prosecution using the Proceeds of Crime Act.

> **Case study: Joint Prosecution using the Proceeds of Crime Act**
>
> A landlord, who amassed a property empire by illegally putting 28 flats into four houses, was prosecuted and ordered to pay £303,112 under the Proceeds of Crime Act. The London Borough of Brent brought the prosecution using evidence from planning enforcement officers from both Brent and Harrow Councils. This demonstrated to Magistrates how the landlord had flouted planning regulations in both boroughs.

> The two planning enforcement teams pooled their resources to use the Proceeds of Crime Act. The landlord concerned had failed to comply with planning enforcement notices against a number of properties. The £303,112 was a confiscation order based on rent collected from tenants who lived in the properties from 2005. On top of the £303,112 confiscation order under the Proceeds of Crime Act, the landlord was ordered to pay a fine of £7,515 for the breach of the planning regulations and legal costs of more than £18,000. HM Treasury received half of the fine and the rest was divided between Brent and Harrow Councils, Brent and Harrow Trading Standards, and the Court Collection Agency.

Deterring Rogue Landlords

V. Given the time and cost of prosecutions, local authorities will want to consider doing all they can to deter rogue landlords and raise public awareness – both so that the public report any properties of concern and so that prospective tenants are informed about landlords to avoid. Local authorities should consider –

- Naming and shaming prosecuted landlords. Some local authorities have done this very effectively – see the case study below. In many areas there are particular shops or newspapers which advertise accommodation so these are useful to target with any publicity materials.

Oxford Case Study – Naming and shaming prosecuted landlords

Getting publicity for prosecutions is essential for sending out the message to landlords, agents and tenants that local authorities will use their powers where necessary. A range of media options was used by Oxford City Council to maximise the publicity opportunities offered by successful prosecutions of criminal landlords. The Council:

- Held Media training courses for officers, including TV interview techniques
- Developed relationships with newsroom contacts in local media organisations
- Agreed to publish successful prosecutions as the lead news item on the Council's website
- Included prosecution cases in the Council's newspaper which is sent to every household in the city
- Issued press releases and photos to a wide audience of media, including newspapers, radio and TV as well as specialist professional publications
- Included details of prosecutions in quarterly newsletters sent to landlords
- Included case studies of prosecutions at landlord training events

What was the result?

- Local newspapers published the full details of prosecution cases – they particularly liked good photos
- The newspapers followed up the issue and ran several in depth features on what steps the Council was taking to deal with criminal landlords
- Public comments on the newspapers websites on articles about prosecutions were overwhelmingly positive
- The prosecution articles got picked up by news agencies and spread around the specialist media, particularly those who are web based
- A TV company approached the Council to film officers taking action against criminal landlords for a trailer for a documentary series
- The names of landlords and letting agents prosecuted by the Council became well known by the others operating in the sector and it damaged their reputation and businesses
- The Council developed a reputation as a strong enforcer who targeted the non-compliant

- Making it clear who the public should contact to raise concerns. This could be as simple as issuing a leaflet or holding an open day for people to raise concerns. An example of publicity material provided by Slough is below.

- Making sure tenants are clear about their rights. In 2011, DCLG published "Top tips for tenants" which provides a short and simple summary of tenants' rights and responsibilities. This is free to download. Local authorities can also work with other advice services, and with landlords and letting agents to ensure that tenants have the information they need. Links are provided in the useful links and contacts section of this document.
- Landlord accreditation schemes can be effective in raising the standard of accommodation available locally. Around 70% of local authorities currently have some sort of scheme.

Example Publicity Material

We Are Here To Help

In recent years there has been an increase in the number of what we call 'Slough Sheds'. You may have heard about these on the radio or read about them in the local newspapers. 'Slough sheds' are usually converted garages or out-buildings in gardens used as sleeping accommodation. They often lack sanitation, have dangerous electrics and are in contravention of the Planning laws.

The Council has set up a special group of officers to inspect these "Sheds" to ensure that the health of the occupiers is not being put at risk. Officers have been targeting areas in Slough and inspecting sheds since the beginning of the year. During the week beginning **28th June 2010** we will be visiting houses on and around the **Farnham Road area** (Please see the map on the other side of this leaflet).

Council officers will be in the Church café on Sunday 27th June after the 12 noon mass to answer any questions you might have about these inspections or general queries concerning renting accommodation in Slough. Or alternatively you can contact the Private Sector Housing Team on:
☎ 01753 875264

Slough
Borough Council

Conclusion

Local authorities have a range of powers they can use to tackle the issue of rogue landlords in their area. Effective working with local partners is critical to addressing the serious problems that rogue landlords can inflict on communities and the hardship that can be suffered by tenants. In particular, where a local authority suspects that illegal activity is associated with problem properties they should work closely with other agencies to address this. It is also very important that criminal landlords are brought to justice and that those contemplating tenant exploitation are aware of the penalties that can be brought to bear against them. Better information for tenants and support for reputable landlords can also help to ensure that rogue landlords do not have the opportunity to exploit vulnerable people.

Further information

DCLG:

Top tips for tenants: Assured shorthold tenancies: http://www.communities.gov.uk/publications/housing/tips tenantsassuredshorthold

Housing Health and Safety Rating System: Enforcement Guidance: Housing Act 2004 Part 1: Housing Condition: http://www.communities.gov.uk/publications/housing/housingact2

Health and Safety ratings system – guidance for landlords and property related professionals: http://www.communities.gov.uk/documents/housing/pdf/150940.pdf

Housing Health and Safety Rating System: http://www.communities.gov.uk/documents/housing/pdf/142631.pdf

Further advice on planning enforcement can be found at:

Circular 10/97 Enforcing Planning Control: Legislative Provisions and Procedural Requirements: http://www.communities.gov.uk/publications/planningandbuilding/circularenforcingplanning

Circular 2/2005 Temporary Stop Notice:
http://www.communities.gov.uk/publications/planningand
building/circulartemporarystop

Circular 2/2002 Enforcement Appeals: Procedures:
http://www.communities.gov.uk/publications/planningand
building/circularodpm enforcement

And on undertaking Article 4 Directions at:
http://www.communities.gov.uk/documents/planningandb
uilding/pdf/1759738.
pdf

UK Border Agency
Further information for potential Assisted Voluntary Return Applicants and others may be found on:
www.refugee-action.org.uk

Refugee Action can be contacted on 0808 800 0007 (free from mobile phones as well as land line)

Other UKBA guidance is available on:
http://www.ukba.homeoffice.gov.uk/sitecontent/document
s/policyandlaw/modernised/returns/assisted-voluntary-
returns.pdf?view=Binary

For regional links and contacts:
http://www.ukba.homeoffice.gov.uk/aboutus/your-region/

Police

Information on Police Powers can be found at: http://www.homeoffice.gov.uk/police/powers/

Find your local Police team / Service information at: http://www.police.uk/

Local Government Association

The Private Sector Housing Forum on the Local Government Association's Knowledge Hub website provides local authorities with the opportunity to share information about private sector housing issues:

https://knowledgehub.local.gov.uk/group/privatesectorhousingforum

ANNEX A – LOCAL AUTHORITY POWERS

Local Authorities have a wide range of powers to tackle the problems associated with criminal landlords. These powers have been enhanced by the Localism Act 2012. This summary also includes information on the relevant powers held by other bodies.

Power	What the power allows	What the power can deliver
Housing 2004 Act	Housing Health and Safety Rating System is an evidence based system used to assess housing conditions in all residential property. The Housing Health and Safety Rating System sets a minimum standard for all residential properties, ensuring that they are safe and habitable. The Housing Health and Safety Rating System comprises an assessment of the presence and severity of 29 hazards, including 'excess cold'. Local authorities have a duty to take enforcement action to secure necessary improvements where Category 1 (serious) hazards are	A local authority can carry out an assessment of a home and will look at the likelihood of an incident arising from the condition of the property and what the harmful outcomes might be.

As a result of the assessment, the council will be able to say whether the property has 'Category 1' (serious) or 'Category 2' (other) hazards.

If the local authority discovers serious Category 1 hazards, they will first discuss these with the home owner or landlord to encourage them to deal with the problems. If this isn't successful, then they can:

· serve a hazard awareness notice to draw attention to the problem |

		present. Local authorities also have discretionary power to intervene where Category 2 hazards are present. In determining the most appropriate form of action, local authorities can consider the extent of vulnerability of persons living (or likely to live) in the accommodation.	· issue an improvement notice to the landlord to carry out improvements to the property· take emergency action to fix the hazard where there is an immediate risk · ban the use of the whole or part of a dwelling or restrict the number of people living there using a prohibition order · If a home owner/landlord doesn't carry out the requirements of a legal ('statutory') notice issued by the local authority, they could face a fine which is currently up to £5,000 but will be increased to unlimited when the Legal Aid Sentencing and Punishment of Offenders Act is commenced.
	Mandatory Licensing in Houses OF Multiple Occupation	There is a statutory duty on local authorities to license larger higher risk Houses in Multiple Occupation of three or more storeys housing five or more unrelated persons. These properties are seen as higher risk, both because of the nature and condition of the properties, and the	Private landlords must be deemed to be a "fit and proper" person in order to be granted a licence. Local authorities can impose conditions on a license, such as how the license holder deals with the behaviour of occupiers and the maximum number of occupants allowed in the property. They can also impose conditions requiring

	vulnerability of their occupants. The mandatory Houses in Multiple Occupation licensing regime addresses poor management practices and aims to secure a reduction in death and injury from fire and other health and safety hazards, and ensures adequate provision of amenities.	adequate amenities and safety requirements to ensure decent standards in properties where there are several households sharing basic facilities. Breach of a licence condition is an offence currently subject to a fine of up to £5,000. Letting or managing a property without a licence is a criminal offence currently subject to a maximum fine of £20,000.
Additional Licensing IN Houses OF Multiple Occupation	Poor conditions and bad management practices can manifest themselves in smaller Houses in Multiple Occupation in specific areas. These smaller types of Houses in Multiple Occupation may not meet the mandatory licensing criteria but there is a discretionary power to extend licensing to smaller types of Houses in Multiple Occupation. Local authorities have the general consent to introduce such schemes subject to local consultation.	In order to introduce additional Houses in Multiple Occupation licensing schemes local authorities are required to consult with local residents, landlords and tenants for a minimum of ten weeks. Local authorities are required to provide a robust evidence base for introducing a scheme, such as demonstrating there are significant management issues and poor property condition that need addressing within a designated area. Once a designation is confirmed landlords who

		operate within the designated area will be required to apply for a Houses in Multiple Occupation licence for each of their properties.
Selective Licensing	This is a discretionary power to license all privately rented properties in a designated area that is deemed to suffer from low housing demand and/or significant and persistent antisocial behaviour. Such schemes are subject to local consultation. Selective licensing is intended to address the adverse impact that poor management by a minority of private landlords, and antisocial behaviour by a few tenants, can have on other tenants and the wider community. Selective licensing is only concerned with the management of privately rented property, not property condition.	In order to introduce a selective licensing scheme local authorities are required to consult with local residents, landlords and tenants for a minimum of ten weeks. Local authorities are required to provide a robust evidence base for introducing a scheme, such as demonstrating there are significant management issues that need addressing within a designated area. Once a designation is confirmed landlords who operate within the designated area will be required to apply for a licence for each of their properties.

Special Interim Management Orders	This is a power to take over the management of individual privately rented properties which give rise to significant problems of anti-social behaviour if the landlord does not take action to deal with the problem. Local authorities can use this power to tackle serious anti-social behaviour emanating from individual privately rented properties that are causing problems for the local community, without the need to introduce a selective licensing scheme.	Local authorities will require approval from a Residential Property Tribunal in order to make a Special Interim Management Order. In order for it to be granted the local authority will need to demonstrate that a private landlord is failing to address the anti-social behaviour and that the Special Interim Management Order is necessary to protect the health, safety and welfare of occupiers, neighbours or visitors to the property. Once in force, a Special Interim Management Order will last for a period of up to twelve months.

Local authorities will take over the management of the property from the landlord i.e. will collect rent, do repairs, spend money from rents on its management functions etc. |

Planning legislation

Under powers in the town and country planning act 1990[1], local planning authorities have wide-ranging, discretionary enforcement powers to deal with breaches of planning control. The powers provide for a controlled and proportionate response to a wide range of breaches of planning control. Ultimately failure to comply with any enforcement action will lead to the courts, and it will be for the courts to decide what sanction to impose.

1 As amended by the Planning and Compensation Act 1991, the Planning and Compulsory Purchase Act 2004 and the Localism Act 2011.

Power	What the power allows	What the power can deliver
Planning Contravention notices	This may be used where it appears that there may have been a breach of planning control and the local planning authority require information about the activities on the land or to find out more about the nature of the recipient's interest in the land.	Penalty for non-compliance is a level 3 fine (maximum £1,000) on summary conviction. A second conviction for continuing noncompliance can be penalised by a daily fine. A false or misleading response to a Planning Contravention Notice (either deliberately or recklessly) is subject to a penalty of a level 5 fine (maximum £5,000) on summary conviction (s171D Town and Country Planning Act 90).
Temporary Stop Notices	This stops any activity for a period of 28 days. This allows the local planning authority time to decide whether further enforcement action should be taken.	Penalty for non-compliance is a fine of up to £20,000 on summary conviction or an unlimited fine on indictment (s171G Town and Country Planning Act 90).

Enforcement notice	This notice requires steps to be taken to remedy the breach within a given period (there is a right of appeal to the Secretary of State against an enforcement notice).	If the notice is upheld, the penalty for failure to comply is a fine of up to £20,000 on summary conviction or an unlimited fine on indictment. If non-compliance continues after conviction, a further conviction can result in a daily fine. In determining the amount of the fine, the court "shall in particular have regard to any financial benefit which has accrued or appears likely to accrue to him in consequence of the offence" (s179 Town and Country Planning Act 90).
Stop notice	This has the effect of immediately stopping any activity which contravenes planning control guidelines and where there are special reasons which justify doing this. A stop notice can only be served with or subsequently to an enforcement notice. It cannot prevent the use of a building as a dwelling house.	Penalty for non-compliance is a fine of up to £20,000 on summary conviction or an unlimited fine on indictment. A second conviction for continuing non-compliance can be penalised by a daily fine. In determining the amount of the fine, the court "shall in particular have regard to any financial benefit which has accrued or appears likely to accrue to him in consequence of the offence" (s187 Town and Country Planning Act 90).

Breach of Condition notices	This can be issued where there is a failure to comply with any condition or limitation imposed on a grant of planning permission.	Penalty for non-compliance is a level 4 fine (maximum £2500 from 6 April 2012). A second conviction for continuing noncompliance can be penalised by a daily fine (s187A Town and Country Planning Act 90).
Injunctions	Injunction in the High Court or County Court to restrain any actual or expected breach of planning control (including against someone whose identity is unknown.	Non-compliance is a contempt of court and can be penalised by a fine or possibly imprisonment.
Powers of entry	Powers of entry on to land are available for authorised officers of the local planning authority for the purposes of obtaining information required for enforcement purposes. Wilful obstruction of an authorised person is an offence.	An authorised person can enter land at any reasonable hour but must give 24 hours' notice to enter any building used as a dwelling house (s196A Town and Country Planning Act 90). If the entry has been refused or the case is urgent, entry under a warrant issued by a Justice of the Peace may be authorised at a reasonable hour (s196B Town and Country Planning Act 90). This offence is a general one for Town and Country

			Planning Act 90 and is not specific to enforcement. The penalty is a level 3 fine (maximum £1,000) on summary conviction (s325 Town and Country Planning Act 90).
Article 4 Directions		Article 4 directions allow local planning authorities to withdraw the 'permitted development' rights that would otherwise apply by virtue of the Town and Country Planning (General Permitted Development) Order 1995 as amended. An article 4 direction does not prevent the development to which it applies, but instead requires that planning permission is first obtained from the local planning authority for that development.	Domestic outbuildings can often be erected without the need for specific planning permission from the local council (i.e. as permitted development). However, this cannot allow outbuildings for the purposes of primary living accommodation. It is possible to withdraw permitted development rights and instead require that planning permission is obtained through making 'article 4 directions'. Such directions must go through local consultation.

Other indirect means of redress

The landlord may have breached other areas of law and as such it may be appropriate to work with the Serious

Organised Crime Agency to bring action against the perpetrator.

Power	What the power allows	What the power can deliver
Proceeds of Crime Act	If a defendant has been convicted of a listed serious offence or has a history of a number of convictions, the court can assume that all their property is the proceeds of crime and can be factored into the amount of a confiscation order. Confiscation orders are made through the Crown Court. Although there is power under the legislation to make confiscation orders in Magistrates Courts this has not yet been commenced. The Proceeds of Crime Act allows specific financial investigation powers which are also available to civilian investigators in the public sector (known as accredited financial investigators). The National Policing	The Act provides for: · The confiscation of the value of the proceeds of crime following any criminal conviction regardless of the amount; · The freezing of assets from the beginning of an investigation so as to prevent their dissipation; · Civil recovery: a process that allows for the Serious Organised Crime Agency and the main prosecution agencies to effectively sue for the proceeds of crime in the High Court. This is against property, rather than an individual, and so does not require a criminal conviction; · Seizure and forfeiture of cash (not less than £1,000) which is the proceeds of, or intended for use in crime; · Serious Organised Crime Agency to tax the suspected proceeds of crime. In 2010-11 Local Authorities

| | Improvement Agency has the lead on training, accrediting and monitoring financial investigators. Over 20 bodies have investigators and there are 119 Accredited Financial Investigators within the Local Authorities. This allows accredited financial investigators within local authorities to apply for restraint orders, to seize and seek the forfeiture of suspect cash and investigate the suspected proceeds of crime. | recovered assets to the value of £4.45m (and they were paid back £2.4m under the Asset Recovery Incentivisation Scheme). The cases referred to Serious Organised Crime Agency for civil recovery action resulted in £900,000 being recovered. |

ANNEX B – POWERS OF OTHER AGENCIES

UK BORDER AGENCY

1. The UK Border Agency has a number of powers to execute its functions, and maintains information on non-European Economic Area nationals who have entered the country lawfully or previously been dealt with as an immigration offender. Immigration officers have the power to arrest and detain non-European Economic Area nationals committing offences under the Immigration Act 1971, both at ports and inland. Immigration officers' more limited powers over citizens of the European Economic Area and their family members are currently governed by the Immigration (EEA) Regulations 2006.

2. The power to detain immigration offenders is exercised as a last resort and is for the purpose of effecting the person's enforced removal from the UK. It can sometimes take some time to manage a person's removal because of the need to obtain the necessary travel documentation from the relevant overseas government, and the need to address legal challenges. The UKBA prefers that illegal migrants leave the UK voluntarily at their own expense. Where appropriate, UKBA provides assistance for illegal migrants to facilitate a dignified return through Assisted Voluntary Return, schemes.

   a) Voluntary Assisted Return and Reintegration Programme is open to asylum seekers or failed asylum seekers of any nationality (apart from UK, European

Economic Area or Swiss nationals) meeting eligibility criteria relating to criminality, immigration history and status in the UK.

b) Assisted Voluntary Return of Irregular Migrants assists irregular migrants – illegal entrants, trafficked people, smuggled people, overstayers – of any nationality (apart from UK, European Economic Area or Swiss nationals) to return to their country of origin. It is not open to those who are been in the asylum system.

c) Assisted Voluntary Returns for Families and Children this programme provides specific assistance for returning families and also to unaccompanied children (under-18). It is open to those who have sought asylum or are irregular migrants. A family is considered as one or two parents or legal guardians and at least one child under-18. Any other family members over 18 may be considered under the Voluntary Assisted Return and Reintegration Programme or Assisted Voluntary Return of Irregular Migrants as appropriate, or make a Voluntary Departure through UKBA. Each individual family member under Assisted Voluntary Returns Families Children is eligible for reintegration assistance of up to £2000 including a £500 relocation grant on departure and, once home up to £1500 in kind. UKBA may, in certain circumstances, meet the cost of departure in cases where evidence of the persons inbound carrier is not available. Departure in these circumstances will not include any element of assistance payment. It should be noted that the above programmes are dependent on cooperation from the person's home government authority for travel documentation. Speed of departure is therefore reliant on that countries administrative processes.

The Author

HMO Daddy Jim Haliburton is a star of the BBC show *Meet the Landlords*, author of over ten books and manuals including *How to Become a Multi-Millionaire HMO Landlord*, and regularly writes articles for property magazines.

He began investing in property in 1991, letting rooms to students, while he was a college law lecturer.

In 2004, he decided to leave his job and buy investment properties full-time. He now owns a letting office as well as over 100 HMOs, thirty single-lets and has twenty-four Rent-to-Rents.

He is also in regular demand as a speaker at property meetings around the UK, and runs courses and mentorships on the business of being an HMO landlord. He is unique in the business in that he lets people work in his property business to learn the skills of being an HMO landlord and gives tours of his properties.

I Want to Hear from You

As a reader of my book you are the most important critic and commentator. I value your opinion and comments. I would like to know what else you would like me to include in the book and what you disagree with. Also, any other words of wisdom you wish to make.

I welcome your comments and you can email, call or write to me to let me know what you did or did not like about my book as well as what I can do to make my book better, or what other information or service I could provide. Please note that I am often difficult to contact by phone because, as you can appreciate, I am very busy. But when I get a few spare minutes I love to talk about the business so please do not be offended if I say call back or leave a message.

If you are interested in finding out more, I also provide training courses on all aspects of my business, which you can find out about on my website www.hmodaddy.com.

When you write to me please include your name, email address, home address and phone number. I assure you I will value and review your comments.

Email: jim@hmodaddy.com

Website: www.hmodaddy.com

Mail: Jim Haliburton
            14 Walsall Road
            Wednesbury
            WS10 9JL

Phone: 0121 531 5137